Words at Work

David Horner
Peter Strutt

CAMBRIDGE
UNIVERSITY PRESS

Published by the Press Syndicate of the University of Cambridge
The Pitt Building, Trumpington Street, Cambridge CB2 1RP
40 West 20th Street, New York, NY 10011–4211, USA
10 Stamford Road, Oakleigh, Melbourne 3166, Australia

© Cambridge University Press 1996

First published 1996
Printed in Great Britain at the University Press, Cambridge

ISBN 0 521 43872 1 Book
ISBN 0 521 43873 X Cassette
ISBN 0 521 58534 1 CD

Contents

Map of the book

Thanks and acknowledgements

The authors and publishers are grateful to the following companies and individuals who have given permission for the use of copyright material in the text:

pp. 25, 43, 44, 80, 81: *Cambridge International Dictionary of English*, Cambridge University Press, 1995; p. 26: the Gleneagles Hotel and the International Conference on Strategic Marketing; p. 33: Holiday Inn and Hyatt Hotels; pp. 32, 41, 80, 81: *The Oxford Advanced Learner's Dictionary*, Oxford University Press, 1995, by permission of Oxford University Press; p. 37: Books for Children, Time Life UK, Dixon's/Currys Ltd, *SHE* magazine © National Magazine Company, Tesco Stores Ltd, Trendex Ltd; p. 38: McDonald's Restaurants Ltd, Mercedes-Benz U.K. Ltd, Shell U.K. Ltd; the Apple logo which appears on p. 38 is reproduced by kind permission of Apple Inc. © Apple Inc., all rights reserved; p. 93: chart reproduced by kind permission of Midland Bank plc.

The authors and publishers are grateful to the following illustrators and photographers:

pp. 6, 11, 28, 37, 47, 53, 65, 95, 106: Jeremy Pembrey; pp. 12, 19, 24, 59, 72: 'Alex' cartoon by Charles Peattie and Russell Taylor © 1988, published by Headline PLC; p.28 (flight attendant): John Davis; p. 34: Zefa pictures; p. 51: drawing by Dana Fradon, © 1977 The New Yorker Magazine, Inc.; p. 72: cartoon by Sophie Grillet; p. 97: drawing by O'Brian, © 1975 The New Yorker Magazine, Inc.; p. 101: Koby Fishman.

All other illustrations and book design by MetaDesign London.

The authors and publishers would like to thank the following people involved in the production of the audio cassette:

Cassette produced by James Richardson and engineered by Jerry Peal at Studio AVP, London. Actors: Tim Bentinck, Carole Boyd, Andrew Branch, Denica Fairman, Michael Fenton-Stevens, Nigel Greaves, Dominic Hawksley, Juliet Prague, Jill Shilling.

Introduction to the learner

How to use this book

This book consists of:

- an introductory unit on learning vocabulary successfully
- 17 theme-based units
- an answer key
- an index of key vocabulary with phonetic transcriptions

A cassette with recordings of the listening tasks is also available.

We recommend you work through the introductory unit called *Learning vocabulary successfully* first. It will give you good ideas on how to approach vocabulary learning and increase the number of words you remember.

Look at the map of the book to see which areas of business vocabulary are dealt with. Then you can choose in which order you want to work on the units.

You may also want to choose different aspects of vocabulary to focus on (e.g. opposites, prefixes and suffixes, using a dictionary and so on).

Types of task

Some types of task appear regularly in the units. These include:

Pronunciation. We believe it is very important to learn how to pronounce vocabulary correctly. For this reason every unit contains at least one pronunciation task. In addition, of course, you should do your best to learn to pronounce all the vocabulary correctly. Phonetic transcriptions are given in the index at the back of the book.

Related words. This section appears in most units. It contains tasks and exercises on words which are associated with the topic of the unit in some way.

Word grammar. Words don't only have meaning; they also have grammar, and successful use depends on knowing this grammar. This section deals with things such as verb patterns and countable/uncountable nouns.

Word partners. This section deals with words that are often found together. There are no rules for this; such combinations are the result of history. So there is no secret – you will have to learn them by heart.

Word building. Under this heading we deal with the way new words are created in English. This section includes, for example, work on prefixes and suffixes.

Synonyms and opposites. This section provides practice in recognising and using words of more or less similar or opposite meanings.

Linking words. These are words which join sentences together. They express ideas like contrast, sequence, cause and effect.

Easily confused words. Learners frequently confuse many pairs or groups of words in English because, despite their differences in meaning, they are closely associated with each other. This section deals with such problems as *personal/personnel*; *remind/remember*; *trip/travel/journey*, etc.

Learning vocabulary. Every unit contains a section with advice on how to store, remember and extend your vocabulary.

Most units contain at least one listening task to give you the opportunity to hear the vocabulary as well as see it. Don't worry if you don't understand everything on the cassette when you first listen. If you can do the task you have been successful. You can always turn to the tapescript if you want to study it in greater detail.

The key

Answers to the tasks can be found in the key beginning on page 107. You will also find the transcripts of the listening tasks.

The index

The purpose of the index is to enable you to:

- find words you want to look at in the units
- see how words are pronounced

The cassette

This contains all the listening tasks marked ▭. There are many kinds of task and you will hear a variety of accents (both native and non-native speakers).

Self-study

If you are working on your own:

- Read the section on page four called *Understanding and using vocabulary* very carefully and try to carry out its recommendations.
- Try to work on your English every day. It is better to do a little on a regular basis than a lot occasionally.
- Establish priorities. What do you need to work on now? What can be left until later? Use the map of the book and the index to help you.
- Find a friend or colleague you can work with and/or practise your new vocabulary with. (You can perhaps do this over the phone, by fax or e-mail.)

Using dictionaries

Some of the documents in English which you receive may contain a lot of words you don't know. But if you look up *every* unknown word in a dictionary, you can waste a lot of time and soon become discouraged. Sometimes the dictionary is not necessary, as enough of the meaning of the word can be worked out from the context.

On other occasions you will have to use a dictionary. When you want to use a monolingual dictionary we recommend:

Cambridge International Dictionary of English
Longman Dictionary of Contemporary English
Collins COBUILD Dictionary of English
Oxford Advanced Learner's Dictionary

Many of you will also want to use a bilingual dictionary. However, we suggest you invest in one which is comprehensive. Avoid small pocket dictionaries, because they do not contain enough information.

Learning vocabulary successfully

Understanding and using vocabulary

It is particularly important to make a distinction between the vocabulary which you only need to *understand* and the vocabulary which you need to *use*.

If you just need to recognise and understand a word or expression when you see it or hear it, then you only need to know its meaning (or meanings!) and its form (spelling and/or pronunciation). But if you want to use a word, then you need to know much more. You should know:

- the meaning (e.g. a *sponsor* is a person or organisation that helps pay for an event such as an exhibition or sports competition.)
- how a word is pronounced (/ˈbɪznɪs/) and spelt (b-u-s-i-n-e-s-s)
- its grammar (e.g. to depend *on* or to depend *of*? to succeed *in* or to succeed *to*? Can we say *a travel* or *informations*?)
- its collocations, i.e. the words it is often found with (e.g. we say *a closing date* but not *a shutting date*; we *clinch* a deal, *settle* an account, *draw* a conclusion, etc.)
- its connotations, i.e. its positive or negative associations (e.g. a *cheap* product may be good for the consumer because it is inexpensive. But the word *cheap* may also be used to indicate that the product is of poor quality.)
- the differences in meaning and use between one word and another related one (e.g. what is the difference between a *firm*, a *company*, an *enterprise* and a *venture*?)
- the translation, if there is one that is appropriate

Often, when studying a language, we don't think about learning all this information.

For example, how much information can you supply about the following words?

1 **invoice**   (Noun or verb or both? What other word(s) can you place before this word?)

2 **suggest**   *to suggest <u>to</u>? to suggest <u>that</u>? to suggest + verb + ing?)*

3 **visit**   (Noun or verb or both? Which of these words – *undertake*,
                  perform, *make*, *pay* – frequently combine with it?)

4 **thrifty**   (What does this word mean? Does it have positive
                  associations?)

5 **mean**   (What does *mean* mean? Can it be used as an adjective?
                  If so, does it have positive or negative associations?)

6 **famous**   (Positive or negative associations?)

7 **notorious** (Positive or negative associations?)

Filing and storing words

A It can be very easy to forget vocabulary you have just learnt. So
people often try to write words and phrases down or record them in
some way. Here are some places where they may put them:

- on pieces of paper or cards
- in an exercise book
- in the textbook they are using
- in an alphabetical index
- in an electronic dictionary

Do you know any other ways? Which do you think is the most useful?

B The idea of a database can be useful for storing vocabulary.
A vocabulary database could look like this:

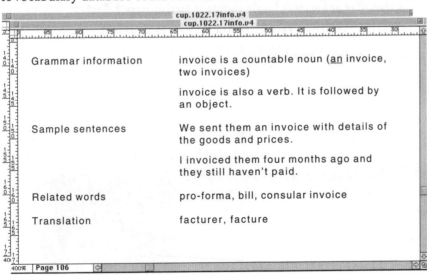

Very often it is the RELATED WORDS field which is the most
difficult to fill. Think of a well-known word like *meeting*:

- In English there are many related verbs (*to call* a meeting, *to hold*
  a meeting, etc.).
- How many related verbs can you give in your native language?
- How many of them do you know in English?

Ideas for filing words

Here are some suggestions for storing words and testing yourself. Choose one you think would work for you. Do you have a better system you already use?

'I'm very organised, so when I meet new vocabulary that I think will be useful to learn I write it on a card together with any important grammatical information about it and an example sentence. And I write the Swedish translation on the other side. I keep new words in a folder and learn them for about 15 minutes every day. When I think I've learnt a word I put the card in a shoebox of words that are related – I have about 12 different shoeboxes now! Once a week I go through a couple of my shoeboxes and test myself again. When I'm sure I know a word, I write it in my private dictionary and throw the card away.'

Birgitta Nyberg (Sweden)

'I have a programmable electronic dictionary that I add every interesting word to. I always have it in my briefcase and when I'm travelling on business I make a point of testing myself: first by just the translation, then by writing the word in sentences.'

Julián Gonzáles (Argentina)

'I keep an alphabetical notebook, with one column in English and another in Korean. I always have it in my pocket and when I have time I get it out and fold the page in half and test myself, sometimes English–Korean, sometimes Korean–English. Any word I don't know I write in the back, where I keep a special section of words that I need to work harder on.'

Joo Young Park (Korea)

Setting objectives

People are very good at forgetting things. So it is a good idea to review vocabulary you have studied. And it is better to do a little often than a lot occasionally.

How many words can you learn in an hour? An afternoon? A month? When is the best time to learn them? Look at the following list and decide which times would suit you best on a regular basis.

- before going to work/college
- during working hours
- during the lunch break
- after work
- at the weekend
- while travelling to work/college
- while travelling on business
- other times (which?)

How will I know I have learnt the vocabulary?

In the business world there is only one real test. Can you use this vocabulary when you need it in your job? Although some vocabulary stays easily in the mind, some doesn't, so we suggest that you try to find opportunities to use the words as often as you can, either at work or outside.

A learner contract

You have thought about your objectives and the time you have available, and you know what learning vocabulary involves. So now think about the following questions and then set out your vocabulary-learning goals.

- *What* words do I need to review?
- *How* shall I revise them?
- *When* shall I do it?
- *How* long shall I spend doing it?

Be as realistic as possible. You are making a contract with yourself, so there is no reason to be dishonest. We encourage you to take your contract seriously.

We hope you enjoy using the book. Good luck.

1 Company organisation

1 Related words: Organisations and occupations

A What kind of organisation do you work for or want to work for?

- the state
- a private limited company
- a nationalised company
- a partnership
- a public limited company
- other

B Is your own past, present or future position included in the list below? If not, what is your profession? Do you think you are in the right post? What would you like to be doing in five years' time?

Jobs	Industries	Divisions
I'm a/an	I work in	Finance
administrator	chemicals	Advertising
executive secretary	advertising	Sales/Marketing
business student	computers	Accounts
receptionist	manufacturing	Human Resources
computer programmer	information services	Public Relations
supervisor	telecommunications	Logistics
financial consultant	electronics	Research and
Vice President	insurance	Development
Managing Director		
switchboard operator		

2 Pronunciation: Syllable stress

Listen to the recording. Write the words you hear and indicate the stressed syllable(s). For example:

. ■. . .
administrator

Now listen again to the recording and repeat the words.

█3 Easily confused words: *personal/personnel*

A Which of these two words means 'belonging to a particular person'? Which means 'people employed in a company'?

B How are they pronounced?

C Fill in the blanks with either *personal* or *personnel*.

1 Does your Managing Director have a .... assistant?

2 Does your company have a .... Department or a Human Resources Division?

3 We weren't able to offer the new service because we hadn't got enough trained ....

4 Do you agree that you shouldn't mix your .... and professional life?

█4 Talking about corporate structure

A Listen to a senior executive talking about the structure of a major chemicals multinational and complete the organigram below with the names of the divisions.

```
                        ┌─────────────┐
                        │  President  │
                        └─────────────┘
```

| 1 .... | 2 .... | 3 .... | 4 .... | 5 .... |
| Vice President | Vice President | Vice President | Vice President | Vice President |

| 6 .... | 7 .... | 8 .... | 9 .... | 10 .... |
| Vice President | Vice President | Vice President | Vice President | Vice President |

B Find the words in the snake which correspond to the description of each division or department.

1 It buys in supplies.

2 It sends out invoices and receives payment.

3 It organises in-house courses for employees.

4 It finds out whether or not a product will sell.

5 It checks the accounts.

6 It ensures that the product reaches dealerships and wholesalers.

7 It organises the manufacturing process.

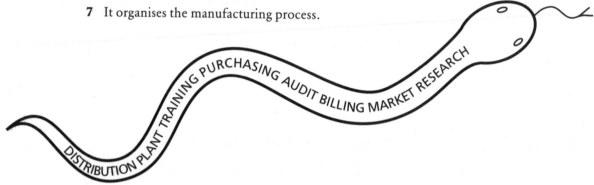

DISTRIBUTION PLANT TRAINING PURCHASING AUDIT BILLING MARKET RESEARCH

C Explain the corporate structure of a company you know well and draw an organigram.

■ 5 Word partners: Verbs and prepositions

A Listen again to the recording of the senior executive talking about corporate structure (Task 4A). As you listen, match the verbs in box A to the prepositions in box B.

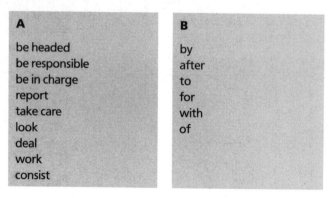

A	B
be headed	by
be responsible	after
be in charge	to
report	for
take care	with
look	of
deal	
work	
consist	

B Now use the above verbs and prepositions to describe your own work relationships.

6 Easily confused words: *subsidiary/agency/branch*

A Match the definitions to the words above.

1   A business or place of business providing a (usually specified) service.

2   A local office belonging to a national firm or organisation.

3   A company which is controlled by a parent company.

B Put the right word – *subsidiary*, *agency* or *branch* – into the blanks.

1   Coca-Cola has a(n) .... in more countries than there are in the United Nations.

2   A travel .... can organise business trips as well as holidays.

3   A(n) .... is a company of which more than half the share capital is owned by the holding company.

4   The major banks have at least one .... in all large cities.

7 Learning vocabulary

One of the best ways of remembering words is by meeting them all the time. One business person we know uses Post-its™ to do this:

'Every time I come across a new word that I want to learn, I write it on a Post-it™. Then I stick the Post-it™ somewhere in my flat. They are stuck everywhere – on furniture, doors and walls – my favourite place is in the kitchen. Then, every time I go past one of my Post-its™, I try to remember what the word means, and imagine a context I could use it in. It may not always look very nice and tidy, but I learn a lot of words that way.'

Josianne Peccoud (France)

Branch

Subsidiary

Organisation

Agency

2 The right person for the job

1 Related words: Applying for a job

A How many different ways of *finding* a job can you think of?

B Look at these job advertisements. Take particular notice of the words and expressions used to describe the post, the company, the responsibilities, the profile of the ideal candidate and the remuneration. Make notes on each advertisement, as in the example below for the post of Private Secretary in Brussels.

The title of the post	Private Secretary
The type of company	successful company in the financial sector
The responsibilities described	business and personal affairs of the Chairman; secretarial services to other directors
The type of person required	pleasant, well-educated, flexible, articulate, numerate; must have integrity and a warm personality
The business skills required	excellent typing, WP and shorthand
The pay and benefits	negotiable salary, subsidised staff restaurant, medical insurance

PRIVATE SECRETARY
Brussels – Salary negotiable

You will be dealing primarily with the business and personal affairs of the Chairman of this successful company in the financial sector but will also provide secretarial services to other directors.

This post calls for a pleasant, well-educated, flexible, articulate and, above all, numerate person (25+) with excellent typing, WP and shorthand skills.

Integrity and, most importantly, warmth of personality are also essential requirements. Candidates should be experienced at Board level, preferably in the financial sector. A non-smoking policy is operated within the offices.

Fringe benefits include subsidised staff restaurant and medical insurance.

Write, with CV,

EUROPEAN ACCOUNTANT

Amsterdam £40–45,000 Dutch Florin equivalent + quality car

This fast-expanding public company is a group of European businesses in ten countries serving distribution and manufacturing industry throughout the EU, Scandinavia and Eastern Europe. The main activities of the group are contract hire, equipment sales and leasing.

Reporting to the chief accountant, you will be responsible for a team of four people involved with assets, cash and company control. This will include the preparation of annual budgets and forecasts together with advice on potential acquisitions.

The person we wish to appoint will need to be competent, disciplined and computer-literate.

This post is an opportunity to move quickly into a senior position and the initial rewards package includes excellent salary, pension scheme, and generous relocation assistance.

South-East Asia Marketing Co-Ordinator
Graduate 25 –30

Singapore-based

Clay & Moore, a leading consultancy in the field of business and information management, is seeking a Marketing Co-ordinator to serve the needs of major national and multinational clients.

He/She will play a key role in the newly-formed S.E. Asia Marketing function and carry specific responsibility for advertising and public relations. Duties include developing promotional literature, making presentations, and working with the network of national marketing co-ordinators.

As such, extensive travel throughout the Pacific Rim is required.

A good university degree is essential and a solid background in a marketing environment.

The ideal candidate will be fluent in at least one Oriental language. Annual earnings not less than £40,000 p.a. equivalent + profit-sharing and usual perks. If you are looking for a challenging career in a stimulating environment send your full CV to:

SALES DIRECTOR

For the Brazilian subsidiary of a major international manufacturer of cash registers and point-of-sale systems.

We are recruiting a high-flying professional who will report directly to the Chief Executive. He/She will further expand our already substantial market share in Brazil and play a major role in increasing our sales effort in Latin America.

The person we require is likely to be 35/40 years of age, dynamic, hard-working and motivated, and with a proven track record in selling business equipment.

An excellent remuneration package is available including profit-related bonus, company car, and substantial salary.

Write in full confidence to:

2 Synonyms: Job advertisements

In each of these sentences a word or phrase is missing. Without
looking back at the advertisements, decide what could go in the
blanks. Then check your answer with the words and expressions
used in the ads.

Example
Annual earnings not less than £40,000 p.a. + profit-sharing and usual
perks/fringe benefits.

1 We .... a high-flying professional who will
   further expand our already substantial market share.

2 This post .... a pleasant, well-educated, flexible,
   articulate and, above all, numerate person.

3 The person we require is likely to be 35/40 years of age, dynamic and
   motivated, and with .... in selling business equipment.

4 .... developing promotional literature, making
   presentations, and working with the network of national marketing
   co-ordinators.

5 Clay & Moore, a .... consultancy in the field of
   business and information management, is seeking a marketing
   coordinator.

6 He/She will .... role in the newly-formed
   marketing function.

3 Pronunciation: Word stress

Contrast the pronunciation of the following words. Indicate where
the stress falls.

Nouns	Verbs	Adjectives
present	present	present
	perfect	perfect
record	record	
permit	permit	
transfer	transfer	
reject	reject	

Check your answers with the recording. Then listen again and repeat
the words.

In general, how does the stress differ when two-syllable words are
used as nouns, adjectives or verbs?

■4 Word building: Adjective formation

Look at these adjective endings (all the words are in the advertisements on page 13).

consider<u>ate</u>	creat<u>ive</u>	responsi<u>ble</u>
challeng<u>ing</u>	dynam<u>ic</u>	success<u>ful</u>
compet<u>ent</u>	motiva<u>ted</u>	

A Using these adjective endings, how could you describe someone who shows:

commitment	flexibility	promise
confidence	imagination	skill
energy	independence	tact
enterprise	power	talent

B How would you describe someone who can:

count .... ate
read .... ate
speak well .... ate

■5 Word building: Compound adjectives

Many adjectives are made up of two parts:

good-tempered   (adjective + noun + -*ed*)
low-paid, newly-formed   (adjective or adverb + past participle)
fast-expanding   (adjective or adverb + present participle)

**The two parts of these words have been jumbled.
Put them together again.**

1	far-	educated
2	fast-	lasting
3	hard-	reaching
4	high-	working
5	long-	thinking
6	well-	flying

6 Pronunciation: Adjective endings

Look at the following adjectives ending in -*ic*, -*ible* and -*ate*.
Notice which syllable is stressed.

energetic   flexible   considerate

dynamic   sensible   articulate

responsible   numerate

As you can see from the ▪ ■ symbols, we can formulate rules for
words with each of these endings. For example:

Words ending in -*ic* are stressed on the second-to-last syllable.

Now write rules for words ending in -*ible* and -*ate*.

What about words ending in -*able*? For example, *capable*, *adaptable*?

7 Personal skills

Look at the job advert below. What *personal skills* do you think would
be necessary?

Step into the magical world of The Cartoon Adventure Park

You can enter this enchanted kingdom today, with its
five different 'adventure-lands' and twenty-nine
fascinating attractions: its shops, restaurants and six
'themed' hotels. This is a unique environment in which
you can apply your skills to the entertainment and well-
being of all our guests.

RETAIL MANAGER
10-15 stores, 100-150 staff

You will play a central role in the development and
success of a chain of retail outlets in the theme park and
in the hotels.

Key tasks will include the recruitment, training and
motivation of your team, working with them to build an
expanding profitable business. You will also be
responsible for ensuring The Cartoon Adventure Park's
world-famous standards of service.

8 Job specifications

 A Now listen to a conversation between two people who are preparing the specification for the job in Task 7. Make notes on the kind of person they are looking for.

B Write a job advertisement for the post you currently hold or would like to hold. Make sure to give details of the responsibilities and the profile of the ideal candidate.

If you do not work, write an advertisement for a position you would like to apply for.

9 Learning vocabulary

When noting down the vocabulary you learn, it is a good idea to write not just the word itself but also other words which are grammatically related. In this way, you can build up tables like the following one (which you can complete).

Nouns	Verbs	Adjectives
subsidy	subsidise	subsidised
benefit		beneficial
	prove	proven
success	succeed	
promotion		promotional
	expand	expanding
		promising
	please	
		innovative

3 Pay and perks

1 Priorities

What motivates you (or would motivate you) in a job? Put the following list in your order of preference:

- the kind of work you do
- the freedom to act on your own initiative
- a sense of achievement
- the opportunity to be creative
- the chance to travel
- prestige
- a high salary
- financial security
- other things (which?) ....

2 Easily confused words: *salary/wage(s)/ earnings/income/revenue/fee/perks/ fringe benefits*

A Look at the dictionary extracts and complete the tree diagram on the next page.

1 **Salary** /'sæləri/ money paid monthly directly into a bank account, normally to professional people and office workers.

2 **Wages** /'weɪdʒəz/ money paid weekly and usually in cash, normally to manual workers.

3 **Earnings** /'ɜːnɪŋz/ a) the total of the sums earned by an employee during a regular pay period. b) what is left of the net profit of a business after allowing for transfers to reserves.

4 **Income** /'ɪnkəm/ money we receive from work, investments, etc. It can be earned income (wages or salary) or unearned income (money from dividends, interest, royalties, etc.).

5 **Revenue** /'revənjuː/ a) income, generally the total income earned by the state or a large corporation; it is not used for people. b) money a government receives through taxation.

6 **Fringe benefits** /'frɪndʒ, benɪfɪts/ (*famil.* perks) extras such as a car or free accommodation received by right in addition to a wage or salary.

7 **Fee** /fiː/ a payment to a lawyer, doctor, etc. for professional services.

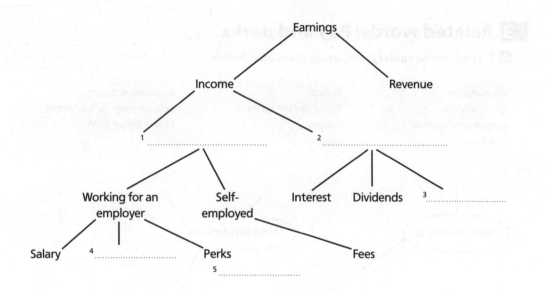

B Complete the sentences using the appropriate word.

1 How much .... did you earn on your shares last year?

2 Our company offers very good .... : a company car, expense account and so on.

3 The best lawyers often ask for the highest ....

4 The machine operators have asked for another rise in their weekly ....

5 Total company .... for 1996 was the best yet.

6 My total .... this year, including salary, royalties, fees, dividends and perks, should exceed £300,000.

C Think about the situation in your country. What words do you use for these terms in your language?

▐3 Related words: Pay and perks

A Complete the spidergram, using the words below.

commission	bonus	expense account
company car	share option scheme	private medical insurance
luncheon vouchers	wages	low-interest loan
overtime	salary	

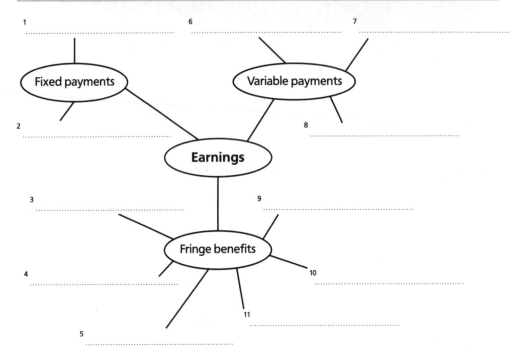

B Add any others you think are useful.

C How are these people usually paid?

a factory worker
a sales representative
a senior manager
an executive secretary

▐4 Pronunciation: Linking

A Listen to the recording. Notice how these compound words are linked.

expense account	/eks'pensəkaʊnt/
life assurance	/'laɪfə ʃɔːrəns/
share option scheme	/'ʃeə ˌrɒpʃən'skiːm/
low interest loan	/ˌləʊw'ɪntrəst'ləʊn/

When this linking occurs, is the sound at the end of the first word a consonant or a vowel? And what about the sound at the beginning of the second word?

Now listen again to the recording and repeat the words.

B Mark the linking in these compounds (be careful, not all of them have linking):

job sharing	unearned income	per annum
medical insurance	company car	performance-related pay
share income and dividends	executive secretary	sales representative
	head office	

 Check your answers to B with the recording. Then listen again and repeat the words.

5 Performance-related pay

A What do you understand by (1) performance-related pay? (2) appraisal?

B

1 List any advantages and disadvantages of performance-related pay you can think of.

2 Which employees should it apply to? All, or only some? (Which?)

3 Who should do the appraisal?

4 How long do you think it should take to implement such a system in a department which doesn't already have one?

5 Would you expect people to be in favour of or against the introduction of performance-related pay?

6 What would you do with people who are not performing as well as expected?
   a dismiss them
   b arrange an appraisal meeting to plan improvements in performance
   c cut their salary
   d reduce their workload

7 What can be done to make appraisals objective?

 C Now listen to an interview with the senior partner in a firm of chartered accountants and see if her answers to the questions in B are the same as yours.

■6 Easily confused words: *raise/rise*

Note that in British English an increase in salary is called a *rise*.
In American English it is called a *raise*.

A The verbs are more easily confused. Look at the following
sentences and decide which verb – *raise* or *rise* – is transitive (can
have a direct object) and which is intransitive (cannot have a
direct object).

1   The government has raised social security contributions again.

2   Income tax has been raised.

3   The cost of entertaining clients is rising.

4   Wages have risen.

B Put the correct form of *raise* or *rise* in the sentences.

1   Prices .... considerably last year.

2   Salaries are expected to .... by 4 per cent next year.

3   Tax cuts have .... real income.

4   The number of workers participating in the profit-sharing scheme
    has .... due to increased profits.

C Talk about what has risen or been raised recently in your country
or work situation. (Mention pay, inflation, (un)employment,
investment, etc.)

■7 Related words: Conditions of employment

Look at the words in the box below and the letter at the top of the
next page. Complete the letter with appropriate words from the box.

appointment	remuneration package
medical insurance	scales
paid leave	starting salary
rise	terms and conditions
performance-related bonus	under review

Dear Mr Escobar,

I am very pleased to offer you an [1] .... with our company at our head office in Cambridge.

The overall [2] .... will include a [3] .... of £40,000 per annum plus full use of a company car and free [4] .... In addition, it is the company's practice to pay a [5] .... to all staff on 30 November each year. Salary [6] .... are currently [7] .... and it is expected that a five per cent [8] .... in salary will be payable as from 1 April. You will be entitled to five weeks' [9] .... per year.

This offer is subject to the attached [10] .... of appointment.

◼ 8 Learning vocabulary

In this unit you completed a tree diagram in Task 2 and a spidergram in Task 3 to show how one general word can be sub-divided into more specific words, or to illustrate how words are related to a general topic.

Try to produce a similar spidergram for the word *taxation*.

Think about other words you know. Draw spidergrams but do not fill in the topic word. Show your network to a colleague, who should then guess the missing word.

4 Travel

1 Reasons for travelling

A Why do you (or your colleagues) travel on business? Put the following in order of importance:

- to attend conferences
- to go on training courses
- to attend in-company meetings
- to visit clients
- to liaise with suppliers

- to visit agents or dealers
- to visit manufacturing plants
- other reasons (say what they are) ....
....
....

How often do you or they travel?

B Now listen to four businesspeople talking about their business trips. Fill in the grid as you listen.

	Reasons for travelling	**Frequency**
Speaker 1		
Speaker 2		
Speaker 3		
Speaker 4		

Alex

I FEEL DREADFUL... THIS IS WORSE THAN I EXPECTED.

I KNOW IT'S A BIT ROUGH

BUT IT'S ONLY A SHORT FLIGHT.

I'M REALLY SORRY, CLIVE...THIS IS SO EMBARRASSING. I THINK I'M GOING TO HAVE TO AVAIL MYSELF OF THE SICKBAG...

NO NEED TO APOLOGISE, ALEX.

I THINK YOU'RE DOING JOLLY WELL, CONSIDERING THIS IS THE FIRST TIME YOU'VE TRAVELLED ECONOMY CLASS.

I'LL NEVER LIVE THIS DOWN...

2 Easily confused words: *trip/travel/ journey/tour*

These words are often confused. Read the extracts from a learner's dictionary and complete the sentences below with the appropriate word.

trip [JOURNEY] /trɪp/ *n* [C] a journey in which someone goes to a place and returns from it and which usually takes a short time or involves travelling a short distance • *The trip from York to Newcastle takes about an hour by train.* • *Do you want to go on the school trip to France this year?* • *I thought we might hire a motorboat this afternoon and take a trip* **round/around** *the bay.* • *(esp. Br) I don't think we can afford another trip* **abroad** *this year.* • *On a warm sunny day there are few things more pleasant than a gentle boat trip down the Thames.* • *I'm afraid she's away on a* **business** *trip and won't be back until next week.* • *She has had to cancel her trip because of illness.* • *He disappeared during a* **fishing** *trip in Scotland.* • *We hoped she'd be with us for Christmas, but she was too weak to* **make** *the trip.* • *It's a 10-mile trip from the airport to the city centre.* • *His visit to Rome will be his first trip* **overseas** *since he became prime minister.* • *I was thinking we might go on a* **shopping** *trip to Oxford on Saturday.*

trav•el /ˈtræv•ə/ *n* [U] *air travel* • *space travel* • *business travel* • *We share a love of literature, food and travel.* • *Since 90% of the country is jungle, travel is not easy.* • *It said on the travel* **news** *that there'd been an accident on this stretch of road.* • A **travel agent** is a person or (also travel agency) a company that arranges tickets, hotel rooms, etc. for people going on holiday or making a journey. • **Travel expenses** are money that your employer pays you because you are spending that amount on travel which is necessary for your work. • A **travel plug** is one that connects a piece of electrical equipment brought from one country to the electricity supply in another when they cannot be connected directly, used esp. when travelling. • **Travel sickness** (also **motion sickness**) is a feeling of illness, esp. of needing to vomit, which some people get in a moving vehicle. • [PIC] **Plugs**

jour•ney /ˈdʒɜː•ni, ˈdʒɜː•ni•/ *n* [C] the act of travelling from one place to another, esp. in a vehicle • *It's a two hour train journey from York to London.* • *The journey from home to the office takes about 15 minutes.* • *We* **broke** *our journey (=stopped for a short time) in Edinburgh before travelling on to Inverness the next day.* • *Have you had a* **good** *journey?* • *Can I borrow a book to read* **on** *the journey?* • *We crossed the channel via Calais on the* **outward** *journey and Boulogne on the* **return** *journey.* • *Have a* **safe** *journey!* • *The journey* **time** *from London to New York is seven hours.* • *(fig.) As she looked through the old photograph albums, she was taken on a* **nostalgic** *journey back to her childhood.* • *(fig.) He views his life as a* **spiritual** *journey towards a greater understanding of his faith.* • *(fig) Her voyage to India to find out about her family was also a journey of self-discovery.* • (F)

tour /£tʊər, £tɪr, $tʊr/ [C] a visit to a place or area, esp. one during which you look round the place or area and learn about it • *We* **went on** *a* **guided** *tour of/ (Br also)* **round** *the cathedral /museum /castle /factory.* • *A bus took us on a* **sightseeing** *tour of the city.* • *They've just come back from a tour of/ (Br also)* **round** *(=a journey made for pleasure, esp. as a holiday, visiting several different places in) Devon and Cornwall* • *This summer, we're going on a* **walking** *tour of the Swiss Alps / a* **cycling** *tour of Provence.* • *When we went to France, we were accompanied by an English-speaking* **tour guide**. • *Tour* **operators** *(=companies which arrange holidays for people) report that many people are booking their holidays early this year.* • *A tour is also a planned visit to several places in a country or area which is made for a special purpose, such as by a politician or sports team or a group of musicians or dancers or actors: The Queen is* **making** *a two-week tour of Australia.* ○ *The England cricket team is currently* **on** *tour in Pakistan.* [U] ○ *The band is about to begin a* **world** */* **nationwide** *tour.* ○ *She is performing in Birmingham tonight, on the third* **leg of** *(=stage of) her national* **concert** *tour.* ○ *He had to cancel a* **lecture** *tour in the US because of ill-health.*

1   Mr Da Silva is going away on a ten-day .... of inspection of our Asian plants.

2   He told us about his recent business .... to Moscow.

3   She's just put in a claim for her .... and hotel expenses.

4   The flight was fine but the train .... was very uncomfortable.

▇3 Understanding words in context

Read this information on an international conference. Then explain
the words below, using your ability to guess words from context.

venue	delegates	proceedings
fees	refreshments	discounted
reception	refund	

DATES

Tuesday 5 to Thursday 7 November 1995.
The conference opens at 09.30 hrs on Tuesday 5 November and closes at
approximately 16.00 hrs on 7 November.

VENUE

The Gleneagles Hotel, Auchterarder, Perthshire, Scotland.

TRAVEL

Travel can be arranged through International Business Travel, 2nd floor,
Burns House, 48 Waterloo Street, Glasgow G2 7DA. Tel: 44 141 226 2341
or fax 44 141 204 6837. Please quote ref. *International Conference on
Strategic Manufacturing.*

CONFERENCE GALA DINNER

Cocktail reception and dinner on 5 November at 20.30.

FEES

Delegates have the choice of two options:

1 £1,000 + £175 VAT (registration, proceedings, conference, workshop,
    refreshments, accommodation, gala dinner, courtesy coach travel –
    Edinburgh Airport)

2 £750 + £131.25 VAT (no accommodation or gala dinner)

PAYMENT

Cheques payable to <u>Strathclyde Business Centre</u>: ACCESS/VISA.

CANCELLATIONS

must be notified in writing and are subject to an administration charge
(– 50%) before 6 October. Non-attendance = no refund.

PROCEEDINGS

Each presentation in English and a bound copy of the proceedings is
included in the registration fee. Additional copies are available at the
discounted rate of £75 per copy.

4 Pronunciation: Words ending in *-ion*

A Write the missing words in the table.

Nouns	Verbs
accommodation	accommodate
administration	
	apply
	cancel
confirmation	
delegation	
	notify
	opt for
presentation	
reception	
registration	

B Say aloud all the words ending in *-ion*. Where is the stress?

 Check your answers to B with the recording. Then listen again and repeat the words.

5 Related words: Transportation

A Complete the chart with words from the list below. You may want to use some words twice. The first word in each list has been given.

✈	🚗	🚂
boarding card	driving licence (BrE)	platform

baggage reclaim	check-in desk	flight attendant	return ticket
connection	departure lounge	transfer	self-drive
hire	driver's license (AmE)	gate	shuttle
track	driving licence (BrE)	platform	stopover
boarding card	fare	restaurant car	unlimited mileage

Add any other appropriate words you can think of.

B Which person from box A would you expect to say which expressions from box B? (There may be more than one correct answer.)

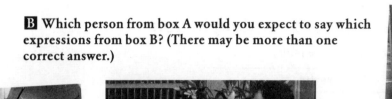

A

cabin/flight attendant	hotel receptionist	travel agent
car rental clerk	mechanic	waiter
conference receptionist	police officer	
customs officer	taxi driver	

B

Are you ready to order now?	It's in the main lecture theatre.
Can I get you anything else?	Red or white?
Do you want full collision protection?	Shall I check the oil?
Have you a clean driving licence?	Shall I put it in the boot?
	Sorry, it's off.
I'm afraid there's no one of that name.	The 4.45 doesn't stop at Coventry.
Are you sure a reservation was made?	What is the purpose of your visit?
It was overheating because the fan belt was loose.	You can't park here.

What other words and expressions about travel would you like to know?

6 Synonyms: British and American English

When travelling abroad, you will often meet people who speak either the British or the American variety of English. There are sometimes different words for the same thing.

Find the pairs of synonyms and put them under the relevant headings. The first two have been done for you.

British English	American English
flat	apartment
puncture	flat

apartment	driving licence	garden	petrol	timetable
autumn	elevator	gas	puncture	toilet
bill	fall	ground floor	rest room	trunk
boot	first floor	lift	schedule	tube
check	flat	motorway	sidewalk	(underground)
driver's license	freeway	pavement	subway	yard

7 Learning vocabulary

One of the ways in which vocabulary is stored in the brain is by related groups. Words which have some kind of connection are kept together in the brain. For example, these words are connected by topic:

conference/delegate/registration/speech

supplier/dealer/delivery/customer

check-in/flight/stopover/shuttle

A Go through the words and expressions you would like to learn in this unit and put them into related groups.

B If possible, compare your groups with some colleagues.

5 Welcoming visitors

1 Related words: Appointments

Find the words in the box which are missing from the sentences below. You can read the words horizontally or vertically.

```
A B P O S T P O N E
C E U D E F T I M E
C A N C E L G H I J
L R C O N F I R M K
A L T L M I N O A P
T Y U Q R X S T K U
E V A R R A N G E W
X Y L A Z K E E P B
```

1 I'm just going to phone Frau Matthies to _____ an appointment for when I'm in Hamburg.

2 'Sorry to _____ you waiting.'
'That's all right, I arrived _____.'

3 Hello, Señor Calpas? This is Helen Slater. I'm afraid I can't be in Madrid on Tuesday, after all. Could we _____ our appointment till the Wednesday?

4 Further to our recent telephone conversation, I am writing to _____ our appointment in Lisbon on 24 May.

5 Have you _____ed a time for your appointment at Lloyds yet?

6 Mr Wang has just called to _____ his appointment for tomorrow, as he has to visit their Malaysian plant.

7 She likes to be _____, because she thinks it's rude to arrive _____ for appointments.

8 In this company, two o'clock means two o'clock, not five past, so I expect you to be on _____ for appointments in future.

2 Customs

A Are there any particular customs which it would be important for a visitor to your country to know about? Note down useful information about:

shaking hands	working hours	smoking
using first names or titles	tipping	religion
appointments	drinking alcohol	

B Sometimes, when travelling abroad, colleagues invite you to their homes. Are there any points of etiquette to remember?

C Which of the following would you expect a guest to do when invited to your home? Which would you expect a guest not to do?

bring flowers	bring something to drink	come with his wife/her husband
bring a cake	belch while eating	phone afterwards to say thank you
arrive early	leave after the apéritif	compliment the cook
smoke	take his/her shoes off	arrive late

Compare with some colleagues. Are there any differences across cultures?

3 Related words: Wining and dining

A What do you understand by the terms *brunch*, *lunch*, *tea*, the *happy hour*, *dinner* and *supper*? At what times of the day do they take place?

B On a menu in the United States or in Great Britain you may see the word *entrée*, but it doesn't mean the same in both places. What does it mean?

C In what order would these words appear on a menu?

appetisers	main courses	beverages
side dishes	desserts	starters

D When eating out, you need to use and understand certain expressions. On the right is a short list. Put the expressions in the right order and use them to write a short dialogue in a restaurant with two diners and a waiter.

E Listen to three people in a restaurant scene. Tick the expressions in D when you hear them. Do they occur in the same order as you put them in? Which do you not hear?

F Often when eating out abroad there are local specialities you don't know. On the recording, for example, Pierre doesn't know what a prawn cocktail is. What exactly does he say to find out? Listen again to the recording.

G Think of some specialities from your country. Describe one.

Could we have the bill please?
Could you tell me what ....
is, please?
Have you chosen?
I'd like .... , please.
What would you like?
Would you like to order?
I'll pay.
I insist.
Do you accept American Express?
Just follow me, please.
Is service included?
We booked a table for ....
in the name of ....
Could we have the wine list?

■4 Easily confused words: *pay/pay for*

Look at the dictionary extract. Which of the following do you *pay*
and which do you *pay for*?

the bill in a restaurant	room service
breakages	a taxi driver
the drinks	a taxi ride
a hotel receptionist	a train ticket
a phone call	a waiter

pay² /peɪ/ *v* (*pt. pp* **paid** /peɪ/) **1(a)** ~ (sb) (for sth): ~ sth (to
sb) (for sth) to give sb money for work, goods, services, etc: [V.
Vpr] *They tried to leave the restaurant without paying (for the
meal).* [Vpr] *Are you paying in cash or by cheque?* ○ *Her parents
paid for her to go* (ie paid the cost of her travel) *to America.* [Vn]
Have you paid the milkman this week? [Vnpr] *How much did you
pay for your car?* ○ *pay sb by the hour/by the job* ○ *Have you paid
that money to the bank yet?* [Vnn] *You haven't paid me the money
you own me.* [Vadv] *My firm pays well* (ie pays high wages). [Vn. to
inf] *You're not paid to sit around doing nothing!*

■5 Related words: Accommodation

A When visiting another place, businesspeople often have to stay
one or more nights at a hotel. What do you look for in a hotel?
Mark what you think is:

- essential
- preferable
- unimportant

good food	a car park	a private bathroom
access to a fax	room service	a central location
friendly staff	cleanliness	a telephone in the room
a double bed	sports facilities	part of a well-known chain
a bar	a fridge in the room	a restaurant open to non-residents
a sauna	conference facilities	proximity to an airport or station

Describe a very good or very bad hotel you have stayed at
or heard of.

B **Where would you expect to hear, see or use these expressions?**

In the event of fire ...
Hello, I've booked a room under the name of ...
I'd be grateful if you could send me up ...
Would you just sign here, please?
Could you add it to my bill, please?
Do you take American Express?
Could I be woken up at 7 o'clock, please?
Could I leave these in the hotel safe?
Could you bring the wine list?
I'm afraid the trout is off.
Draught or bottled?
Guests must vacate the room by 11 a.m.

at Reception

in the dining room

in the lounge

in a bedroom

in the bar

█6█ Word grammar: Multi-word verbs

Multi-word verbs are combinations of frequently-used verbs like *call, come, get, set, turn*, etc. and one or more particles such as *in, on, off, up*, etc.

Sometimes it can be difficult to guess the meaning of a multi-word verb even if you know the meaning of the particles:

We've *taken on* a number of trainees. (= recruited)
Let's *get down to* business. (= start)

Multi-word verbs are common in spoken English as they are used informally in conversation.

You will hear two colleagues talking about a trip to Prague. Read through the questions and listen to the passage. Answer the questions using the multi-word verbs which you hear.

1 What was the trip like?

2 What time did the man and his wife leave for the airport?

3 Where did his wife leave him?

4 What had happened before they separated?

5 What did he do then?

6 What did he do while he was waiting?

7 Who was at the airport to meet him?

8 What did he do next?

9 Why was there no meeting for him to attend?

10 What did he do while he was there?

11 Where did he stay?

12 What does he think of his Czech colleague?

7 Pronunciation: Stress in multi-word verbs

 The stress pattern for multi-word verbs depends on whether they are separable or inseparable. Listen again to how they are pronounced on the recording. Which sort has the stress on the particle? Which sort has equal stress on the verb and the particle?

He offered to put me up for the night.

It turned out to be a total disaster.

There was no one to pick me up.

My wife and I set off for the airport really early.

She dropped me off at the terminal.

Now listen again to the recording and repeat the sentences.

8 Learning vocabulary

You have met a lot of words in this and other units. But it can be difficult to remember and use all these words equally well. Words you think you have learnt one week are forgotten the next.

To help you in your learning, from time to time you can write four columns as below:

I can use these words correctly	I recognise these words but can't use them correctly yet	I think I know the meanings of these words but am not entirely sure	I don't know these words at all

Fill in each column with words from this unit or others you have recently studied. Then come back two weeks later, and read the columns again. Can you move any of the words from one column to another?

6   Advertising

1 Word partners: Compound nouns

A In each of the four lists below only one noun can combine with the other words. Write the appropriate noun in each space.

advertising	brand	market	sales

1
....
name
image
loyalty

2
....
agency
campaign
expenditure
media

3
....
share
research
study
penetration
leader

4
....
forecast
force
drive
promotion
team

B Which of these word partners describes:

1 a product which has the greatest market share?

2 money spent on the promotion of a product?

3 the idea people associate with a product?

4 a special offer to boost sales?

2 Related words: Advertising media

A Look at these forms of advertising. Group them into the two categories, as in the examples below.

cinema
direct mail
hoardings
magazines
newspapers
point-of-sale
posters
radio
sponsorship
television

Inside the home	Outside the home
television	posters

B Which advertising medium is being described in each of these paragraphs?

1 In terms of visual power, this is the strongest medium of all. The combination of a giant screen, multi-track sound and the absence of distractions makes each commercial look and sound better than anywhere else.

2 Most of this is thrown away, though sometimes there is an attractive-looking special offer. But this is probably the sort of thing you don't want in your mailbox.

3 They're designed to catch the attention of the passer-by or the motorist. The picture is usually striking and the catchphrase memorable because there's not a lot of time to read.

4 When it's associated with a major event like the Olympic Games it's good in terms of building up an image and a good reputation but the pay-off may not be immediate.

5 Some have a very wide circulation, but the glossy ones are more expensive. You should choose a good position such as the inside front cover.

6 There could be a video promotion, or advertising material placed on a display stand in the store itself and designed to catch the consumer's eye. In supermarkets there may be product demonstrations or announcements of special offers.

3 Related words: Printed material

Look at the pictures of different examples of printed advertising material. Match them to the names in the box.

catalogue	leaflet
flyer	voucher
insert	

4 Word partners: Compound adjectives

Many of the words used to describe the *features* of a product are
compound adjectives. These are made up of two words joined by
a hyphen. For example: *brand-new*; *record-breaking*.

A These compound adjectives have been jumbled. Try to sort
them out.

1 economy-   purpose
2 multi-   friendly
3 precision- free
4 relief-   saving
5 space-   modern
6 trouble-   size
7 ultra-   giving
8 user-   built

B Which of the above adjectives might describe each of the
following? (There may be more than one answer.)

a lamp	a sports car	medicine
industrial detergent	office furniture	
software	washing powder	

C Can you think of any other product they might describe?

5 Easily confused words: *make/brand/ trademark*

A Which of these are *makes* and which are *brands*?

Marlborough (cigarettes)   Miele (washing machines)

Nescafé (coffee)   Persil (washing powder)

Volvo (cars)   Yamaha (motorbikes)

So what is the difference?

B *Trademarks* are legally registered designs or symbols which only
the owner of the mark may use in connection with the sale of the
goods bearing the mark.

Can you recognise these registered trademarks?

1

2

3

4

6 Pronunciation: Vowel sounds

A Listen to these three sounds on the recording:

/əʊ/	/aʊ/	/ɔɪ/
poster	outlet	point-of-sale

Now listen to the words on the recording. If they contain one of the vowel sounds above, write the word in the appropriate column of the chart. Be careful – not all of them do. Then listen again to the recording and repeat the words.

B The way in which a vowel sound is written may vary, although the sound is the same. For example:

share /ʃeə/   where /weə/

fair /feə/   wear /weə/

On the other hand, the same sequence of letters may be pronounced differently:

coupon /uː/   relief-giving /iː/

voucher /aʊ/   user-friendly /e/

How do you pronounce the following words? Pay particular attention to the vowel sound indicated in bold type.

brand	logo	background
image	money	colour
media	promotion	discount
range	sponsor	journey
slogan	sport	should

Check your pronunciation with the recording. Then listen again and repeat the words.

7 Launching a new product

 Listen to this excerpt from a meeting between Pamela Saunders and
Mark Brown from the advertising agency Johnson & Flew, and Terence
Bride and Martina Makin from O'Reilly's, an Irish manufacturer of
convenience foods. As you listen, complete the extract from the
minutes of the meeting. Pause the recording if you need time to write
the words in.

Minutes of the meeting held at O'Reilly's on 23 March

Present:　Pamela Saunders, Mark Brown (Johnson & Flew)
　　　　　Terence Bride, Martina Makin (O'Reilly's)

MM opened the meeting by stating its purpose: to discuss

1　the overall [1] .... of the [2] ....
2　the [3] .... to be used
3　the length of the advertising [4] ....
4　[5] ....
　　　　　　　　　　　　　　　　　　　　　　　　.

She then invited TB to provide some of the [6] .... to the
[7] ....

TB said that the convenience food market is very complex and fast-
moving and that fashion often influences [8] ....
[9] .... He stated that the firm had done a great deal of
[10] .... and now had a good idea of what the
.... is looking for when purchasing this
kind of product.

He identified four considerations:

1　The product must look attractive;
2　It must be easy to make;
3　It must taste good;
4　The public are ready to spend more on a really
[11] ....

It was thought that the product would be [12] .... and
should [13] .... to both sexes.

As concerns the overall campaign objectives, it was hoped that the
product would [14] .... at least 15% of the Irish and 5% of the
British market within six months of [15] .... Later it would
be launched in mainland Europe and gain a [16] .... there,
despite the [17] .... competition.

MB said that he felt a full TV campaign was needed. However,
unfortunately, [18] .... had been rising rapidly.

MM pointed out that the share of [19] .... on
advertising should be 5% for Britain and 15% for Ireland, roughly
equivalent to the [20] ....

However, it was also maintained that, given that this was a
[21] .... , proportionately more money would have to be invested.

8 Your brief

You work for an advertising agency. Your agency has been commissioned to advertise a new revolutionary language-learning package for businesspeople which accelerates the acquisition process and builds confidence. Think about:

- your objectives
- your initial market research
- the expenditure
- the kind of advertising media you would select
- the duration of the campaign
- the launch
- the market share you expect to obtain

Write a short report describing how you would advertise this product.

9 Learning vocabulary

Dictionaries can give you more information than just the definition of a word. Look at the following dictionary extracts for the words *advertise, advertisement, advertising, publicist, publicity, publicise.*

head word

stress on first syllable

phonetic symbols for pronunciation

v = verb

[I; T] = intransitive, transitive

ad-ver-tise /ˈædvətaɪz‖-ər-/ *v* 1 [I;T] to make (something for sale, services offered, a room to rent, etc.) known to the public, e.g. in a newspaper or on television: *I advertised (my house) in the "Daily News".* |*a big poster advertising a new shampoo*| *Are lawyers allowed to advertise (their service)?* 2 [I (**for**)] to ask (for someone or something) by placing an advertisement in a newspaper, shop window, etc.: *We've advertised for someone to look after the garden.* 3 [T] to make generally known (esp. something that should perhaps be kept secret): *It was unwise of them to advertise their willingness to make concessions at the negotiations.* – **tiser** *n*

note the preposition following the head word

headword + suffix advertiser

ad-ver-tise-ment /ˈədvɜːtɪsmənt, $ˌædvɜːrˈtaɪzmənt/, also ad, ad-vert /ˈvædvɜːt‖-ɜːrt/ *infml*– *n* something used for advertising things, such on a wall or in a newspaper, or a short film shown on a television: *to put an advertisement in the paper /TV adverts in between programmes*| (fig.) *He's not a very good advertisement for the driving school – he's failed his test six times!*

infml= informal usage

fig.= figurative use

ad-ver-tis-ing /ˈædvətaɪzɪŋ‖ -ər-/ *n* [U] the business of encouraging people to buy goods by means of advertisements: *a job in advertising* |*an advertising campaign.*

[U]= uncountable noun

n = noun

pub-li-cist /ˈpʌblɪsɪst/ *n* a person whose business is to bring something, esp. products for sale, to the attention of the public: (fig.) *He's a good self-publicist.* (= he is good at making himself well-known)

pub-lic-i-ty /pʌˈblɪsɪst/ *n* [U] 1 public notice or attention: *The film star's marriage got a lot of publicity.* |*unwelcome publicity* 2 the business of bringing someone or something to the attention of the public: *Who is in charge of publicity for our show?* |*a big publicity campaign to highlight the dangers of smoking*

'unwelcome' collocates with 'publicity'

pub-li-cize ‖ also -cise *BrE* /ˈpʌblɪsaɪz/ *v* [T] to bring to public notice: *to publicize a new policy*

BrE = British English

Look these words up in your own dictionary. Does it give you the same information? Is your dictionary *more* or *less* complete?

7 Getting things done

◼ 1 How do you organise your work?

Complete the following questionnaire.

Questionnaire

1 Which do you tackle first?
  a The job that needs doing? ☐
  b The job you like doing? ☐

2 Do you tend to:
  a leave things to the last minute? ☐
  b work systematically according to your
       action plan? ☐

3 Do you spend a long time:
  a planning and analysing but leave little time
       to take positive action? ☐
  b working hard, only to feel little has been
       achieved? ☐

4 Do you try to:
  a delegate as much work as possible to
       colleagues? ☐
  b do the work yourself because you know
       it will be done well? ☐

5 Do you tidy your desk:
  a at the end of every day? ☐
  b from time to time? ☐

6 Would you say you are:
  a stretched? ☐
  b overworked? ☐

If possible, compare your answers with a colleague.

2 Easily confused words: efficient/effective

ef•fec•tive /ɛɪˈfek·tiv/ *adj* • Something can be described as effective if it produces the results that it was intended to: It's a very effective cure for a headache. ○ The lighting for the production made a very effective use of shadow. ○ A person can also be described as effective if they are skilled in a particular way: She's a very effective teacher. • You can also use effective to mean in fact, although not officially: Although she's not officially our boss, she's in effective control of the office. • See also effective at EFFECT USE • Ⓟ

ef•fi•cient /ɪˈfɪʃ·ənt/ *adj* working or operating quickly and effectively in an organised way • *The city's transport system is one of the most efficient in Europe.* • *We need someone really efficient who can organise the office and make it run smoothly*

Both these words refer to someone or something that works well. But what is the difference? Look at the dictionary entries and then complete the sentences.

1 Mrs Lee is the most .... personal assistant I've ever had – she knows where everything is!

2 Inflation is down from eight per cent to less than two per cent so the government's measures have been pretty ....

3 After a very .... marketing campaign sales were up by 15 per cent.

4 Our despatch department is very.............................. : orders are sent off the same day as they're received.

3 Priorities

Imagine you arrive at work on Monday morning with these tasks to do. Decide which of them are urgent and high priority and which of them can wait. Number them from 1–9 in the order you would do them.

If possible, compare your order with a colleague. Discuss any differences of priority.

Action Pad

* Reorganise the office filing system
* Write the minutes of last Monday's meeting
* Set next year's budget
* Attend the Business English class at 10 a.m.
* Give the director the figures she asked for a week ago
* Call the supplier about discounts on the next delivery
* Write an office circular reassuring staff about redundancies
* Write the agenda for a meeting to be held in 2 weeks' time
* Sign the letters Kathryn typed on Friday

▌4 Word grammar: Verb patterns

There are some verbs which occur frequently when we want to talk about delegating work:

ask	instruct	persuade
get	let	remind
have	make	request
help	offer	require

You probably know most of these words, but you also have to know their *grammar*.

In the above list there are two different verb patterns. For example:

I asked him *to* go.
I let her go. (NOT 'to go')

This kind of grammatical information is given in good monolingual learners' dictionaries.

get *obj* CAUSE /get/ *v* [T] **getting** *past simple* **got** /£ɒt, $gɒːt/, *past part* **got** or *Am. Aus infml* **gotten** /£ˈgɒt·ən/ to cause (something) to be done or persuade (someone) to do something.

help *obj* MAKE EASIER /help/ *v* to make it possible or easier for (someone) to do something, by doing part of the work yourself or by providing advice, money, support, etc. • *Her daughters helped her* **(to)** *carry the table upstairs.* [T + obj + to infinitive]

make *obj* FORCE /meɪk/ *v* [T] *past* **made** /meɪd/ to force (someone or something) to do something • *The vet put something down the dog's throat to make it vomit.* [+ obj + infinitive without to] • *The prisoners are made to dig holes and fill them in again.* [passive + obj + *to* infinitive]

re•mind *obj* /rɪˈmaɪnd/ *v* [T] to make (someone) aware of something they have forgotten or might have forgotten • *Please remind me to post this letter.* [+ obj + *to* infinitive]

re•quire *obj* /£rɪˈkwaɪəʳ, $-ˈkwaɪr/ *v* to need or make necessary • *Working here requires you to have a sense of humour.* [T + obj + *to* infinitive] • *Bringing up children often requires you to put their needs first.*[T + obj + *to* infinitive] • *You are required by law to stop your car after an accident.* [T + obj + *to* infinitive]

have *obj* CAUSE /hæv/ *v* [T] he/she/it **has** /hæz/, *past* **had** /hæd/ to cause (something) to happen or (someone) to do something. • *If you wait, I'll have someone collect it for you.* [+ obj +infinitive without to]

in•struct *obj* ORDER /inˈstrʌkt/ *v* [T] to order or tell (someone) to do something, esp. in a formal way • *The police have been instructed* **to** *patrol the building and surrounding area.* [+ obj + *to* infinitive] • *I've been instructed* **to** *take down the name of everyone present.* [+ obj + *to* infinitive]

of•fer (*obj*) AGREE TO GIVE /£ˈɒf·əʳ, $ˈɑː·fəʳ/ *v* to ask (someone) if they would like to have (something) or if they would like you to do something. • *My father has kindly offered to take us to the airport.* [+ *to* infinitive]

per•suade (*obj*) /£pəˈsweɪd, $pəʳ-/ *v* [T] to make (someone) do or believe something by giving a good reason to do it or by talking to them and making them believe it • *He is trying to persuade local and foreign businesses to invest in the project.* [+ obj + *to* infinitive]

re•quest *obj* /rɪˈkwest/ *v* We request **(of** *the chairman)* that *the next meeting be held on a Friday.* [+*that* clause] • *Visitors are requested not* **to** *walk on the grass.* [T + obj + *to* infinitive] • *(fml) I requested* (= ordered) *a taxi for 8 o'clock.* [T]

A Look at the following extracts and list the verbs according to their grammatical pattern. For example:

get: verb + direct object + *to* + verb

B Make a list of tasks that you have recently dealt with. Are there any you did not do yourself, but delegated to someone else? Are there any that you are often asked to do?

5 Word partners: Verbs and nouns, compound nouns

The words and expressions in this section are useful when talking about a course of action – the initial planning, the anticipation of difficulties and their solutions, putting it into practice and so on.

A Match the verbs in box A with the nouns in box B. Note that there may be more than one possible combination.

A	B
start	a target
reach	a deadline
implement	a decision
troubleshoot	from scratch
meet	progress
deal with	a problem
monitor	
carry out	
handle	

Very often we put two nouns together:

management + objective ┄┄⟩ management objective
company + policy ┄┄⟩ company policy

B Join the words in box A with the words in box B to make compound nouns, and match them to their mini-definitions below.

1 what you finally accomplish

2 a report on what has been done until now

3 the period at your disposal to get something done

4 a first attempt, to see if it works

5 the points you have to bear in mind

6 something you can do as an alternative if things go wrong

7 the day you are aiming to finish

A	B
progress	plan
end	date
time	run
contingency	result
check	report
target	scale
trial	list

6 Preparations and procedures

A Now listen to a woman talking about preparations for a trade fair
and the procedures she follows. As you listen, complete the chart
with these missing stages:

- copywriter produces final copy
- catalogue is printed
- art department produces final layouts
- secretary checks catalogue proofs
- brief art department
- equipment is delivered

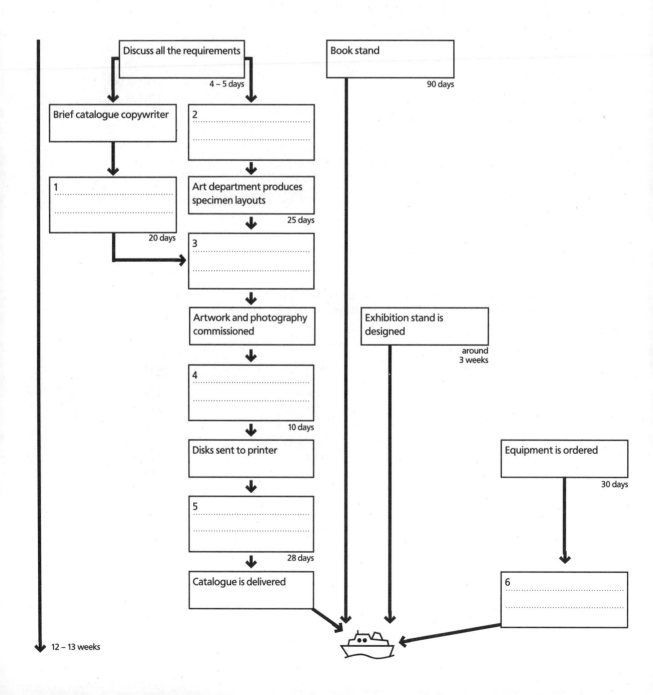

B Now listen again to the recording and fill in the blanks with the words you hear.

1 She's responsible for making sure everything goes ....

2 She draws up a .... and sets herself a ....

3 They need three months' .... to book the stand.

4 She .... the copywriter and the art department.

5 She sets them a ....

6 She monitors .... and .... any problems that might ....

7 Normally, everything goes ....

8 Sometimes they run behind ....

9 She doesn't like leaving things to ....

7 Pronunciation: Consonants

Sometimes words have two or more consonants next to each other. As a result, learners find them difficult to pronounce.

For example, say the following and compare your pronunciation with the words as they are used on the recording:

checked	rushed
hectic	shelved
length	stretched
risks	tasks

Now listen again to the recording and repeat the sentences.

8 Learning vocabulary

'It's the little words I always get wrong, so I decided once a month to work methodically through the new vocabulary I've come across and to sort it according to these little words. I also test myself the same way. For example, I start with a list of all the verbs and adjectives I can think of that are followed by "in" – "believe <u>in</u>", "succeed <u>in</u>", "interested <u>in</u>", "experienced <u>in</u>" and so on.'

Michael Treuter (Germany)

Can you make a list of verbs and adjectives that are followed by *of* and *with*?

8　Meetings

▉1 Reasons for meetings

Ａ Why are meetings held? Fill in the blanks with any words that come to mind:

to communicate ....
to make ....
to plan ....
to pool ....
to settle ....
to solve ....

Ｂ Sometimes meetings are held to take another look at things that were previously decided.

We use the prefix *re-* with certain verbs to indicate that something is being done or considered again. For example:

This meeting has been called to **review** the sales figures in the light of the initial forecasts.

Write a suitable response to the following sentences, together with a suitable verb beginning with *re-*. For example:

A: It doesn't look as if I'll be able to attend Thursday's meeting.
B: OK, we'll have to **rearrange** it.

Use these verbs:

reorder	redraft	reschedule
reconsider	reread	

1 A: I don't think their decision was a wise one.
　　B: ....

2 A: We can't send out a report like that!
　　B: ....

3 A: The meeting can't take place next Monday.
　　B: ....

4 A: We've run out of printer ink.

B: ....

5 A: It's a long time since I looked at the safety regulations.

B: ....

2 Types of meetings

Place the words *meeting*, *committee* or *tank* after the following words.

board ....   sub- ....
steering ....   think- ....

In what ways are these types of meeting different?

3 Organisation of meetings

Which of these do you agree with? Which, in your opinion, is most important and which is least important? Rank them from 1–10.

- hold meetings just before lunch or late in the afternoon
- set a time limit for the meeting to end
- tolerate interruptions and digressions so that everyone has a chance to participate
- circulate essential documents beforehand
- put the most important item in the middle of the agenda
- limit the number of people attending the meeting to eight
- always obtain unanimous agreement
- record decisions and agree on further action
- cancel the meeting if key people or facts are unavailable
- deal with the important issues behind the scenes

4 Word partners: Verb and noun combinations

Match the verbs in box A with the nouns in box B. Note that there may be more than one combination.

A		B	
adjourn	raise	the minutes	an agenda
approve	record	the discussion	something to
draw up	second	a decision	the vote
hold/call	set	a time limit	a motion
implement	table	the proposal	an objection
put	write up	a meeting	

▊5 Setting an agenda

You are responsible for setting the agenda for a meeting. The following items have been submitted: decide in which order you would place them.

☐ Budget for launch of XDLP
☐ Any other business
☐ Apologies for absence
☐ Sales targets for XDLP
☐ Allocation of parking spaces for staff in the new car park
☐ Decision: to launch or not to launch XDLP
☐ Minutes of previous meeting
☐ Results of market research on proposed new XDLP model
☐ Matters arising

▊6 Taking part in meetings

A Listen to the recording. Fill in the blanks with the words and phrases you hear. They are all things people say to introduce a comment they want to make and indicate their opinion.

1 '........................, I don't really understand why we're talking about this now.'

2 '........................ I think it's very important indeed.'

3 '........................, while we're on the subject, I had a phone call from Mrs Chen the other day ...'

4 '........................, I'd be very careful what you say.'

5 '........................, we try to involve everyone in the decision-making process.'

6 '........................! That's what I've been saying for years.'

7 '........................! It just isn't feasible at the moment.'

8 '........................ we're going to have to get together and talk about this in more detail ...'

9 '........................ that's settled. Can we now move on to the next item on the agenda ...'

B Now match these phrases to the words in the box below.

To be frank	In your place	Out of the question
Right	Needless to say	In fact
By and large	By the way	Precisely

C The words you have just heard and read are not at the same level of formality. Which of them are formal? Which are informal? Which are neutral?

■7 Reporting what was said

Read this extract from the minutes of a meeting in which 'just-in-time' procedures are discussed. Then listen to what was said during the meeting and choose the verb which most accurately reflects what was said. The first has been done for you.

Ms Andersson [1] **disagreed with/<u>raised</u>/objected to** the problem of just-in-time supply procedures. While she [2]**questioned/accepted/denied** that they had saved the company a great deal of money in warehousing, she [3] **admitted/claimed/doubted** that they actually caused more problems than they solved. She [4] **added/replied/interrupted** that she believed they had been introduced simply because Japanese management techniques were fashionable.

Ms Deiss [5] **acknowledged/disagreed/maintained** that this was the real reason. She [6] **argued/denied/boasted** that an idea should be judged by its success and that just-in-time procedures had proved their effectiveness by saving money.

Ms Andersson [7] **decided/replied/denied** that they also led to considerable logistical problems due to the large amount of necessary transportation.

Mr Blasetti [8] **admitted/advised/disagreed with** abandoning the use of just-in-time procedures.

The Chairman [9] **admitted/urged/appealed** that it was desirable but doubted whether the solution could be applied.

Ms Deiss [10] **wondered/asked/inquired** whether the logistics problem was as bad as stated.

The Chairman [11] **concluded/encouraged/continued** the discussion at this point and [12] **discussed/recommended/remembered** obtaining further information.

" '_No!_' shouted Mr. Bigsby, slamming his fist down on the table. The floor shook, the walls rumbled. Mr. Watson turned askew. 'Y-y-you m-m-mean w-w-we...' The words wouldn't come out. He seemed to choke on each syllable."

▐8▌ Pronunciation: /e/ /eɪ/ /æ/

A Listen to the pronunciation of the following words. Repeat the words and try to reproduce the vowel sound as accurately as possible.

/e/	/eɪ/	/æ/
trend	raise	plan

B Look at the following words. Put them into three groups: those with an /e/ sound, those with an /eɪ/ sound and those with an /æ/ sound. (The first ones have been done for you.)

/e/	/eɪ/	/æ/
digression	arrange	actually

actually	digression	obtain
arrange	eight	participate
available	fact	raise
cancel	frank	set
circulate	implement	settle
claim	matter	suggest

Check your answers with the recording. Then listen again and repeat the words.

9 Learning vocabulary

Many language learners complain that they always seem to use the
same words. So what can you do to increase your vocabulary store?
One interesting idea we heard about is quoted below.

'I try and identify areas of vocabulary that I'm particularly interested in,
then I go through all the words in that area that I know in Chinese and
see whether I know how to say them in English, too. If I don't, I find out
what the words mean — mostly from dictionaries — but I've got friends
and colleagues at work who speak English too, and sometimes I ask
them. Then I set about learning them. Just by going through all the words
that are in my head, while I'm travelling or in bed or anywhere, but in
English this time. And when I can't remember a word, I look it up again.
I don't learn everything at once, of course, but eventually the
words stick.'

Iris Shen (Hong Kong)

Let's try an example of this technique.
List all the verbs you can think of in your native language which you
can use together with the word for *meeting* in your native language.
There are ten English verbs in the word square. Find them and match
them to your list. You can find the words horizontally or vertically.

C	N	T	A	K	E	P	L	A	C	E
A	J	Q	C	R	E	O	R	P	A	O
R	E	C	G	A	S	S	F	R	L	I
C	H	A	I	R	O	T	P	M	L	A
T	R	E	S	U	S	P	E	N	D	N
G	O	N	E	N	H	O	L	D	C	S
F	E	D	J	C	A	N	C	E	L	I
F	R	S	U	G	G	E	S	T	A	W

9   Budgets and forecasts

1 Keeping to a budget

A Listen to a manager talking about budgets and how they affect her in her job. What is her overall attitude towards the way budgets are set?

B Some of what she says is reproduced below. Listen again to the recording. Write the missing words in the blanks.

> '... often the people who have to work with a budget don't know how it was [1] .... or the reasons why, because they haven't been involved.
>
> ~ ~ ~
>
> ... we're sitting down and informing them about the [2] .... that someone else has decided and telling them they've got to [3] .... these targets without spending more than the sums of money they've been [4] ....
>
> ~ ~ ~
>
> All we have to do is keep to the sums that have been [5] .... for expenditure against the various budget headings – they're not [6] .... if circumstances change, or anything like that. And if the budget is [7] .... we're in a lot of trouble ...'

C Each of these verb pairs can be used with only one of the nouns. Match the verbs and the nouns.

1 earmark/allocate   a target
2 set/revise   costs
3 meet/reach   sums of money
4 hold down/cover   the budget

■2 Pronunciation

🔊 **A** These words have one sound in common. What is it? Listen to the recording and check.

allocate	manager	number
internal	monitor	suppose

Now listen again to the recording and repeat the words.

🔊 **B** Say these words and listen to the recording to check your pronunciation.

accountant	data	quota
analysis	figure	supplies
assess	oppose	
capital	purchase	

Now listen again to the recording and repeat the words.

■3 Synonyms: Updating a budget

A Read through this excerpt quickly (ignore the underlining for the moment). Where do you think it was taken from?

- a company report
- an internal memorandum
- a management textbook
- a newspaper article

Give reasons for your answer.

Budgetary updating is a technique whereby analyses and budgeted information are compared and any [1] <u>variances</u> – due, for example, to over-spending or an over-estimation of [2] <u>requirements</u> – are made the responsibility of certain managers. This constant [3] <u>checking</u> allows managers either to take the necessary [4] <u>remedial</u> action or [5] <u>review</u> the original budgets.

Budgeting is therefore concerned with the planning and control functions of management, which [6] <u>ensure</u> that corporate goals are met. The planning process involves [7] <u>estimating</u> costs and [8] <u>allocating</u> resources in order to [9] <u>fulfil</u> corporate objectives. Budgeting determines in detail how the resources are [10] <u>employed</u> and [11] <u>expenditure</u> [12] <u>planned</u>.

B Now match the words in the box with their synonyms, which are underlined in the passage above.

achieve	guessing	providing
corrective	monitoring	revise
differences	needs	spending
guarantee	programmed	used

▉4 Easily confused words: *check/control*

A Study the sentences. What rules of use do you notice from these examples?

1 'Have you **checked** the figures on the invoice?' 'Yes, I've **double checked** them.'

2 Has she **checked** our expenditure against initial estimates?

3 We're trying to **keep** our spending **in check.**

4 We're trying to **control** our spending by introducing new economy measures.

5 After the takeover they **gained control** of the market.

6 There was a problem but everything is now **under control.**

7 The delay is **due to circumstances beyond our control.**

8 With over 50 per cent of the shares, he has a **controlling interest** in the firm.

B Now complete these sentences, using phrases with *check* and *control.*

1 She's .... the sales results and they are about 5 per cent down on last year.

2 We've been unable to supply for reasons which are

   ....

3 Would you like to .... the documents and see if anything is missing?

4 Even though it has sold off 18 per cent of its shareholding in PCT, the group still has a ....

5 I've .... in the records and they do owe us $500.

6 For a short period we lost .... of the situation.

C In your situation is everything working to plan? How do you know if it is or isn't? What sorts of checks and controls do you make?

5 Word building

A *over-* is used as a prefix: for example, *over-estimation, over-spending*. Which prefix gives an opposite meaning?

B How many verbs can you make using these two prefixes with the following words?

book	pay	value
charge	rate	work
draw	rule	
estimate	stock	

C Which of the words you have made can you use to talk about yourself and things you have done?

6 Word puzzle

Complete the puzzle and find the missing word, which is the theme of this section. You have seen most of these words in this unit already.

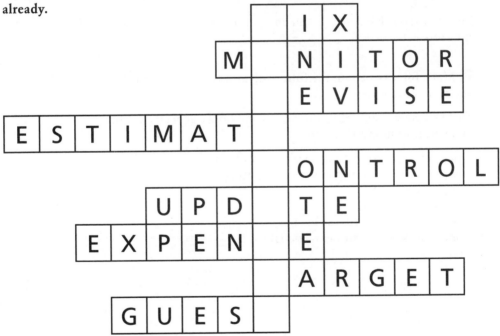

▋7 Synonyms and opposites: Making predictions

Forecasts are about making predictions based on probabilities.
We use a number of adverbs and adjectives to say how probable
or improbable these predictions are.

A Write the words and expressions from the box below on the line
in order of probability.

impossible ──────────────────────────────────── certain

a safe bet	a chance	in all likelihood
unlikely	bound to	likely

Look at how these words are used:

I am	bound to likely to unlikely to	change jobs before the end of the year.

In all likelihood There's a good chance It's a safe bet	our competitors will be cutting their costs.

B Make forecasts about the following events using the words
above. For example:

There's a good chance the government will hold a general election
in the next six months.

- receive an invitation to speak at a conference
- go on a business trip to the United States
- get promoted
- change your job
- be awarded an increase in salary
- exceed your departmental budget

8 Learning vocabulary

Many people play Scrabble™, either on their own or with other people. The aim of the game is to add a word to an existing word on the board, using one of the letters in the word.

Use the grid below to add extra words. Choose words related to the topic of this unit.

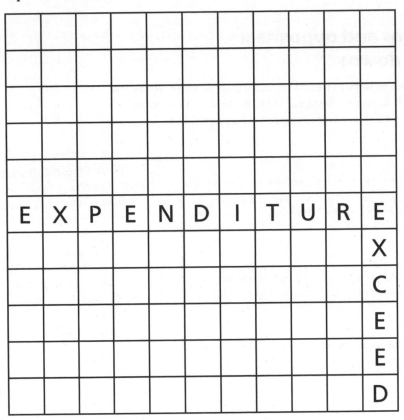

10 Describing change

■1 Synonyms and opposites: Ups and downs

Read the following newspaper extracts and <u>underline</u> the words and expressions which describe change, for example a movement in terms of quantity or price. (The first extract has been done for you.)

A

A <u>sharp fall</u> in natural gas prices is forcing some producers to more than <u>halve</u> production, analysts say.

If the <u>downward trend</u> continues, major companies could temporarily <u>reduce</u> production by as much

as 3bn cubic feet (85m cubic meters) a day by midsummer. Six of the ten largest gas producers said they have already <u>cut</u> production. For example, Seagull Energy Corp has <u>slashed</u> production to 8m cubic feet a day, <u>down</u> from 25m in January.

Spot market gas prices in Texas and Louisiana have <u>dropped</u> to about $1.40 per thousand cubic feet, <u>down</u> from a recent peak of $2.50. Prices could <u>fall</u> as low as $1.30 next month although they are expected to <u>pick up</u> again thereafter.

B

Carlo de Benedetti, chairman of Olivetti SpA, said Thursday that its personal computer shipments had risen sharply. Mr Benedetti said that deliveries should climb to more than 120,000 units this year, compared to 40,000 last year. However, price reductions are still eating into profit margins.

C

Campsa, the Spanish petroleum products monopoly, increased the price of gasoline on Monday by two pesetas. This is the third price hike in the last month, confirming the steady upward trend since the beginning of the year.

D

Radobank Nederland said net profit last year grew by 10% and revenues went up by Fl 0.23bn to Fl 2.78bn.

However, this year the bank expects cost increases to accelerate and margins to come under growing

pressure. Accordingly, it has boosted provisions for general contingencies to Fl 300m.

The bank also reported an advance in the volume of lending despite the unsettled Dutch economy.

E

European car sales plummeted again last month, despite a slight upturn in the economy. Foreign importers continued to strengthen their position, with Japanese producers edging up to third position in France and Germany. The dollar continues to weaken, prolonging the slump in European exports to the US.

2 Synonyms and opposites: Nouns and verbs

A Identify the words in the extracts which can be placed in each of the columns, as in the example.

Verbs		Nouns	
upward	downward	upward	downward
to pick up	to reduce	a hike	a fall

B Which of these words indicate a *strong* movement up or down?

C Look back at the extracts and find the words with the opposite meanings to those in the list below.

1 a rise ....   **5** to rocket ....

2 a loss ....   **6** to dip ....

3 a retreat ....   **7** to double ....

4 a decrease ....   **8** to strengthen ....

D This report does not use a wide enough variety of words. Using those you have met in this section, replace the words in italics.

Sales are divided into three main blocks: North America, Scandinavia and Western Europe. The fourth block, the Far East, [1]*is rising* rapidly, but still has limited significance.

Total US sales [2]*rose* by 11% and a new assembly plant was opened in Detroit. Sales in the Swedish market also [3]*rose* slightly, up approximately 1000 units, and market share [4]*rose* from 19.9% to 21.5%. This result was largely achieved as a result of the success of the top-of-the-range 9000 model, whose sales [5]*rose* by 6%. In Norway, however, the total number of models sold [6]*fell* by 12%, and in Denmark market share [7]*fell* by 1% to 7%. In the Far East, sales [8]*rose* by 15% but market share actually [9]*fell* from 0.8% to 0.6%.

▋3 Synonyms and opposites: Verbs and adverbs

When there is a change, it is also important to describe *how* it takes place. For example:

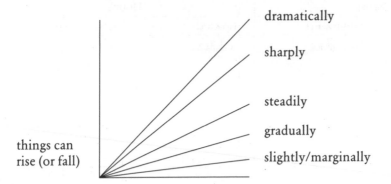

things can rise (or fall)

dramatically

sharply

steadily

gradually

slightly/marginally

A Draw a graph to accompany this paragraph.

> The price of gold rose **slightly** during the first quarter from its turn-of-the-year price (803), but turned up **sharply** towards the end of June and continued to climb until the end of the third quarter, when it fell **marginally**. However, it picked up **gradually** again in November and December and is expected to continue to rise **steadily** in the New Year.

B Which of these sentences do not make sense?

1 Sales of PCs fell steadily throughout last year.

2 Car sales plummeted marginally at the end of June.

3 The price of oil rocketed gradually in 1994.

4 The retail price index edged up sharply at the beginning of the year.

5 Share prices dipped slightly towards the close of trading.

6 The government expects unemployment to continue to fall steadily.

C Adjectives can be used with nouns to describe a change. For example:

a **slight** fall

What other combinations can you make?

4 Prepositions

A Use the correct prepositions from the box to complete the extracts below.

over	at	from	to
under	by	of	

1

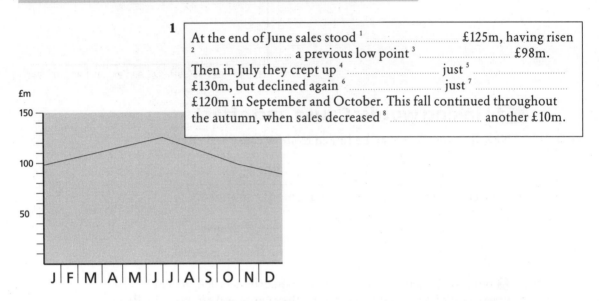

At the end of June sales stood [1] .... £125m, having risen [2] .... a previous low point [3] .... £98m. Then in July they crept up [4] .... just [5] .... £130m, but declined again [6] .... just [7] .... £120m in September and October. This fall continued throughout the autumn, when sales decreased [8] .... another £10m.

2

Germany's biggest metals and engineering conglomerate, Metallgesellschaft, raised net earnings [1] .... 13.2% last year [2] .... $418m, an increase [3] .... $16m. Preliminary consolidated group profits rose [4] .... 9.2% [5] .... $490m after tax.

B Use the first grid to draw a graph showing a company's sales for one year and then describe it to a partner. Your partner should then follow your description and draw it on the second grid in his/her copy of the book.

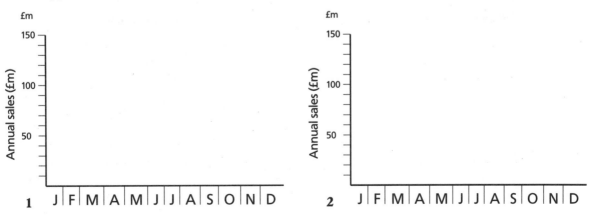

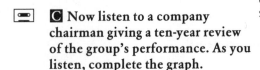 **C** Now listen to a company chairman giving a ten-year review of the group's performance. As you listen, complete the graph.

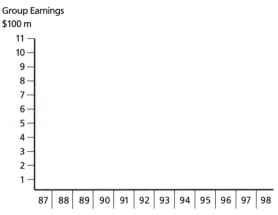

Group Earnings
$100 m

5 Linking words: Cause and effect

Note how sentences can be linked to show cause and effect:

Cause   Effect

Ineffective management *led to* a poor profit performance.

Effect   Cause

The poor profit performance was *due to* ineffective management.

A Now listen again to the chairman's speech in Task 4. As you listen, complete the table by joining the causes and effects. The first one has been done for you.

Effect	Linking words	Cause
1 group earnings rose slightly	*owing to*	the low volume of consumer spending.
2 the low volume of consumer spending		high interest rates.
3 this dramatic slump in profits		some badly-planned diversification moves.
4 earnings began to grow again		some necessary restructuring.
5 this period of zero growth		the prolonged recession.
6 profits slumped again		uncertainty in high-risk countries.
7 the group began to perform well again		the appointment of a new senior management team.

B What changes have there been in your country or situation?
Think about some or all of the following. What caused them?
Try to use the link words you identified in the chairman's speech.

- your company's/department's
  performance
- the rate of inflation in your country
- retail prices

- taxation
- unemployment
- your standard of living
- interest rates

6 Pronunciation: *-ough*

Many English words contain the sequence *-ough*. However, there is
more than one way to pronounce this: /əʊ/ (as in *so*); /ɒf/ (as in *off*);
/uː/ (as in *two*); /ʌf/ (as in *stuff*).

Listen to the recording and place the words in the box under the
correct sound.

although	rough	tough
enough	through	trough

/əʊ/	/ɒf/	/uː/	/ʌf/

Now listen again to the recording and repeat the words.

7 Learning vocabulary

'I use a little game – I call it "word web" – to
revise and expand my vocabulary. For example,
I start with a word like "rise" and then construct
a network of translations and other
related words.'

Anouk Zemmour (France)

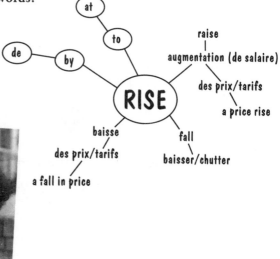

Now do this for your own language, or choose another word.

11   Making presentations

1 Good presentations

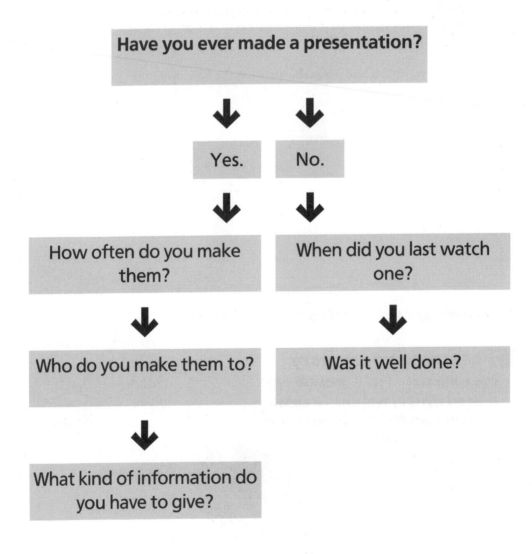

Have you ever made a presentation?

Yes.   No.

How often do you make them?   When did you last watch one?

Who do you make them to?   Was it well done?

What kind of information do you have to give?

So what makes a good presentation?

2 Related words: Visual aids

When making a presentation, a certain amount of equipment is often necessary.

A Match the words in the box to the pictures.

flipchart	transparencies	slide projector
marker pens	pointer	slides
monitor	remote control	video recorder
OHP	screen	whiteboard

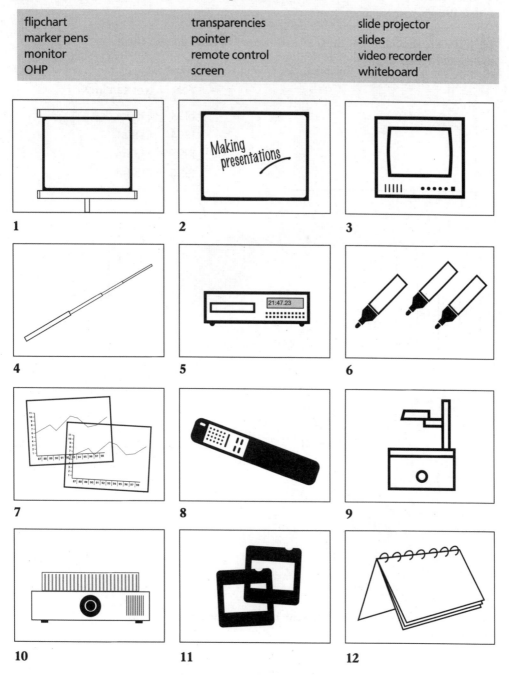

1

2

3

4

5

6

7

8

9

10

11

12

B Which pieces of equipment have you used? Which are the easiest/most difficult/most annoying to use?

▓3 Easily confused words: *diagram/graph/ bar chart/pie chart/scatter chart/table/ pictogram*

When making presentations, you often use different kinds of visual illustrations.

A What are the names of these illustrations? Which do you think have good visual impact?

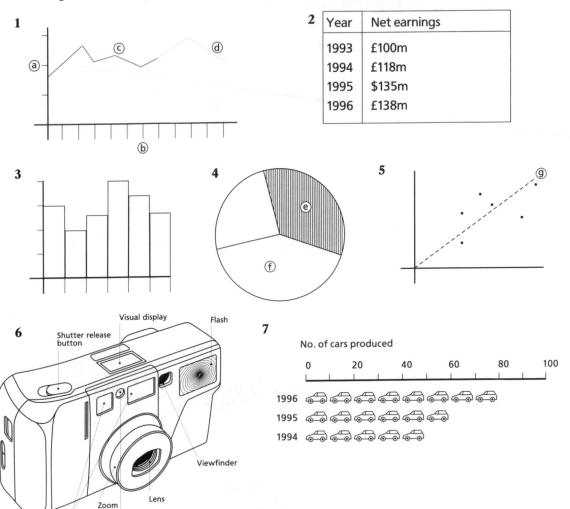

Year	Net earnings
1993	£100m
1994	£118m
1995	$135m
1996	£138m

B Match the words in the box to the letters in the above illustrations.

curve	horizontal axis	segment
broken line	vertical axis	shaded area
dotted line		

4 Pronunciation: Figure work

If you have to make a presentation you will probably have to say
some numbers out loud. Can you say these?

a $^1/_3$ $^1/_2$ $^3/_4$ $^2/_5$

b 0.05   6.25   15–20%   < 90%

c 60 x 3   150 – 40   33 ÷ 3   1:4

d 575   1,001   65,935   7,896,324

Listen to the recording and check your answers. Then rewind the
cassette and repeat each number or calculation.

You may want to refer to *round numbers* rather than highly accurate
figures. So, instead of saying **48.725%**, you could say:

about	
approximately	
in the region of	50%
roughly	
some	

5 Contrasts and comparisons

Presentations often require the making of comparisons – between
one company and another, one year and the next, etc. Here are some
words and expressions which are particularly useful when making
comparisons:

all the same	compared with	on the contrary
although	despite	unlike

This is an extract from a presentation. Put the appropriate
comparison words from the box into the gaps below.

> 'Last year our overall sales figures fell by 18 %, [1] .... they
> had risen steadily in every previous year since 1993. On the face of it,
> this looks bad, but [2] .... our major competitors we are not
> doing so badly at all. [3] ...., no firm can continue for long
> with falling sales, and steps need to be taken immediately if the
> situation is not to worsen.
> [4] .... our fears, domestic sales did rise substantially.
> This is probably because, [5] .... our main rivals, we've
> been able to maintain prices over the last two years while they have
> not. But there is no room for complacency. [6] ...., we
> must continue to renew our efforts to ...'

Listen to the presentation on the recording and check your answers.

6 Linking words: Signalling intention

A Listen to the presentation. As you listen, try to fill in the two
OHP transparencies the speaker displays to her audience.

SIX GOLDEN RULES FOR BUSINESS START-UPS
1 _____
2 _____
3 _____
4 Limit your contractual obligations
5 _____
6 _____

CAPITALISATION	
Sales	£600,000
Gross profit	£ _____
Overheads	£ _____
Profit before interest	£ _____
Interest	£20,000
_____	£60,000

B Now listen again to the recording very carefully. Identify the
expressions which the speaker uses to open and close the
presentation and to invite and answer questions. Add them to the
spidergram below.

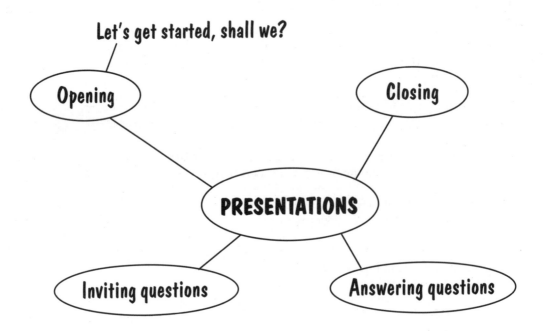

C Add any other expressions you can think of. You can add more
branches if you wish.

D Rewind the cassette and listen again. Which of the expressions in column A correspond to each of the descriptions in column B?

A	B
I'm glad you asked me that. In conclusion … Leaving this aside for the moment … Let me recap on what I've said so far. Moving on to … So … This brings me to my next point … Um … Well …	I'm summing up I'm changing the subject I'm thinking what to say next

7 Making a presentation

Prepare a brief text outlining your company's/department's recent activities. (If you're not in work, use a company report.) Design a visual or visuals to go with it and present it to the rest of the class. Be prepared to answer any questions from the audience.

If possible, video your talk and analyse what you said and how you said it.

8 Learning vocabulary

In Task 6 you saw a spidergram. Spidergrams are also useful ways to identify gaps in your vocabulary and to revise the words you know.

For example, look how the original idea of presentations has given this student ideas for other branches, and how these branches have stimulated the growth of further branches.

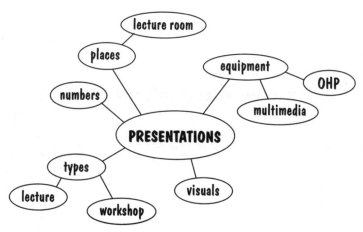

Add more branches or words to existing branches.

12 Personal banking

1 Related words: Banking terms

Hidden in this word square are 13 words to do with banking.
How many can you find? You can read across, down and diagonally.

```
S  C  R  E  D  I  T  Z  S  C
I  A  C  C  O  U  N  T  A  U
G  I  V  S  D  W  B  Q  F  R
N  O  P  I  A  E  I  A  E  R
A  A  A  O  N  V  B  S  C  E
T  N  Y  J  K  G  E  I  E  N
U  S  D  E  P  O  S  I  T  C
R  I  N  T  E  R  E  S  T  I
E  L  C  H  E  Q  U  E  S  E
W  I  T  H  D  R  A  W  L  S
```

2 Related words: Banking services

Banks now offer consumers a variety of
services and have been described as
'financial supermarkets'.

Read the questions in the survey. Make sure you know the meanings of the words in bold. If you can, ask and answer the questions with a colleague. Whose bank gives the best service?

COMPARING BANKS: A CONSUMER SURVEY

1 Does it cost you anything when you **write out** a cheque?
2 Does your **current account** earn **interest**?
3 What is the interest rate on a **savings account**?
4 What is the interest rate for a **personal loan**?
5 Does your bank require **security** for a personal **loan**?
6 How much do you have to pay for a **credit card**?
7 How often do you get a **statement**?
8 Is it easy to get permission for an **overdraft**?
9 Do you have to pay if you want to **stop a cheque**?
10 When, if ever, do you have to pay **bank charges**?
11 How long does it take for cheques to be **debited** or **credited** to your account?
12 If you change money into a **foreign currency** in your branch, do you have to pay a **commission**?
13 If you **withdraw** money abroad from a **cash dispenser** does your bank make a **handling charge**?
14 Is the staff in your **branch** friendly, helpful and efficient?
15 Is there a **home banking** service?

---

3 Word associations

Group these words into ten pairs of related words and explain the way in which each pair is connected. For example:

- *Refer to Drawer* and *bounce*: if a cheque bounces (= is rejected) it is stamped 'Refer to Drawer'.
- *Collateral* and *security* because they are synonyms.

balance	deposit	Refer to Drawer
beneficiary	direct debit	security
bounce	Head Office	standing order
branch	in the red	statement
cash dispenser	overdrawn	Visa
collateral	pay in	withdraw
credit card	payee	

▌4▐ Word partners: Compound nouns

Many banking terms are made up of two nouns, with the first noun used as an adjective to tell us something about the second. For example:

a bank statement: a statement from a bank
a cheque book: a book of cheques
a branch manager: a manager at a branch
a handling charge: a charge which is made for handling

Put the words in box A together with those in box B to create compound nouns (you may want to use words twice). Ask a colleague or your teacher to explain any words you do not know.

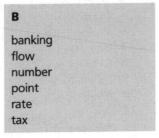

A	B
account	banking
cash	flow
exchange	number
home	point
income	rate
interest	tax

▌5▐ Pronunciation: Word stress

 Listen to the recording and underline the syllables on which the stress falls in the compound nouns you created in Task 4. Then listen again to the recording and repeat the words.

▌6▐ Colour idioms

We have already seen the expression *in the red*. It is not the only idiom using a colour word.

black	green	red
blue	grey	white

Using a dictionary if necessary, complete these sentences with one of these colour words:

1 Reddox plc is a .... -chip company, so your investment is relatively safe.

2 We're not really sure where the responsibility lies – it's rather a .... area.

3 The authorities have given us the .... light and we're now working on the project.

4 With the decline in manufacturing industry there are now fewer
.... -collar workers and more .... -collar
office staff.

5 The discussion on pay scales was a complete ....
herring; we were supposed to be talking about investment.

6 We've no contacts in Ecuador and the order came right out of
the ....

7 In some countries the only way to get spare parts is on the
.... market.

8 The company was saved from a takeover bid by the appearance
of a .... knight.

See if you can find any other expressions associated with a colour.
If possible, explain them to a colleague.

7 Learning vocabulary

If you have to do business translations – and possibly for your own
personal learning – you will want to know how to translate words and
expressions in your mother tongue. To help them do this, many
people keep bilingual wordlists.

Research suggests that this can be a good technique but also shows
that:

- if you want to recall the English word easily for active use, your list
  should have the words in your native language first

but

- if you just want to be able to recognise the English word when you
  see it, you should write the English word first.

Select the words from this unit that you want to be able to use. Then
find their equivalents in your mother tongue. Write the translation
on the left of the page, with the English words opposite them on
the right. Learn the list as quickly as possible and ask someone to
test you.

Wait a few days and then ask someone to test you again.
What percentage were you able to recall?

■8 Banking board game

You need a dice, and a counter for each player.

Rules

- Choose one person to read out the information corresponding to each square. You will have to decide whether the information is good news (you get some money) or bad (you have to pay out).
- Each player begins by throwing the dice. Your opening balance is the figure on the dice x £1,000. You must throw the dice again to make your first move.
- If you land on the **Credit Card** square you have to pay the figure on the dice x £10.
- If you land on the **Standing Order** square you have to pay the figure on the dice x £225.
- On the **Direct Debit** square you pay the figure x £50.
- On the **Stock Exchange** square – multiply the figure x £100. If (1) or (6), debit, otherwise credit.
- On the **Pay Day** square – multiply the figure x £1,000.
- At the end of the game work out how much money you have got left. The person with the most money is the winner.

1 Invoice error of £150 in your favour.

2 £1,500 back pay.

4 Profit-sharing bonus of £750.

5 You buy £800 worth of traveller's cheques.

6 Property tax: £525.

8 Interest rates up. Your mortgage costs £175.

9 Travel expenses reimbursed: £275.

11 Royalty payment of £800.

13 Capital gains tax: £500.

15 Share dividend of £1,000.

16 Legal fees: £1,000.

18 You take out a home improvement loan: £1,750.

19 Income tax rebate of £200.

21 Subscription to a business magazine: £150.

22 Your insurance policy matures: £1,500.

25 Interest on your savings account: £600.

26 A £750 cheque made out to you comes back stamped 'Refer to Drawer'.

27 You withdraw £100 from a cash dispenser.

29 Income tax: £2,000.

30 Interest on your deposit account: £250.

33 News of a takeover bid. Your shareholding in AMIX plc is worth £1,000 more.

34 Your daughter goes on a management training course: £500 fee.

35 Your grandmother leaves you mining shares in her will: £3,000.

37 Collect rent. Dice x £100.

38 A holiday in Rio: £600.

39 Interest rates fall: a saving of £175.

41 A £500 cheque bounces.

42 You sell one of your paintings: £3,000.

44 You make a down payment on a new home computer system: £450.

46 You do some private consultancy work for a fee of £1,000.

49 Quarterly banking charges: £300.

Start ➡	1	2	3 Credit card	4	5	6
						7 Standing Order
32 Direct Debit	33	34	35	36 Credit card		8
31 Stock Exchange				37		9
30		Finish		38		10 Stock Exchange
29		49		39		11
28 Credit card		48 Direct Debit		40 Direct Debit		12 Credit card
27		47 Pay Day		41		13
26		46		42		14 Standing Order
25		45 Stock Exchange	44	43 Credit card		15
24 Stock Exchange						16
23 Standing Order	22	21	20 Credit card	19	18	17 Pay Day

13   Business start-ups

1 Related words: A business plan

Do you know anyone who has tried to set up in business? How is it done? What are the risks? What are the rewards?

A The following extract was written to give advice to people who want to start in business. Read it through and match the headings in the box to each section.

THE FINANCIAL PROJECTIONS	THE PRODUCT
THE POTENTIAL MARKET	THE PROPOSAL

Perhaps you've come into a sum of money or put by some money for a rainy day and now want to put some money into a small business. But how do you go about it? Probably the first thing to do if you feel you are cut out to set up your own business and that your business idea is a good one is to draw up a detailed blueprint.

I would advise the following headings:

1 ....
The plan should begin with a concise overview of your scheme: why it is a sound investment, and how much start-up capital is required. It should set out your scheme in a factual but attractive way. It should bring out the good points but not cover up the risks and must explain how you intend to minimise those risks.

2 ....
Describe it in simple terms: what it is, and how it is used. What is its unique selling proposition? Is it cheaper? Is it better quality? Is it in the R & D stage or is it already patented? What is its likely lifespan? How does it compare to existing competition?

3 ....
Usually it is the sales figures which are most difficult to predict accurately. You will need to describe your target sales territory and define the particular niche in the sector you want to conquer. You should include detailed statistics to back up your findings.

4 ....
The preparation of forecasts is crucial – how many will you sell and when? At what price? Plan your cash flow statements and overheads carefully. Set out your estimated turnover, gross profit margin, net profit before tax and retained earnings.

B Now organise the words below into four groups of three under the following headings:

Proposal	Territory	Financial projections	Expenses

area	forecast	project
blueprint	location	running costs
break-even point	outgoings	scheme
estimate	overheads	sector

2 Word grammar: Multi-word verbs

We often combine frequently used verbs such as *come, cut, get, put, set* with words like *by, in(to), out, up*, etc. These are called *multi-word verbs*.

A There are a number of multi-word verbs in the passage in Task 1. Look through it again and mark the verbs in the grid below. The first has been done for you.

	back	bring	come	cover	cut	draw	go	put	set
about									
by									
into		✓							
off									
out									
up									

Now match the multi-word verbs you have identified in the above passage with their synonyms below. One of them can be used twice.

formulate	highlight	invest	save	suited
hide	inherit	present	start	tackle

B Sometimes a verb can be followed by two particles: for example, *keep up with, put in for, cut down on*, etc.

**Look at the dictionary entries and replace the word in brackets in
each sentence with a multi-word verb (one or two particles).**

come ·up to sth 1 to reach up as far as a
specified point: *The water came up to my neck.* **2** to
reach an acceptable level or standard: *His
performance didn't really come up to his usual high
standard.* ○ *Their trip to France didn't come up to
expectations.*

do a·way with *obj v adv prep* [T] to get rid of or
destroy • *These ridiculous rules and regulations
should have been done away with years ago.*
• *Computerization has enabled us to do away with a
lot of paperwork.* • *How on earth could they do away
with a lovely old building like that and put a car park
there instead?*

run up against *obj v adv prep* [T] to meet
(unexpected difficulty) • *The community scheme
has run up against strong local opposition.*

put up with *obj adv prep* [T] to be willing to
accept (something) that is unpleasant or not
desirable) • *He's finding it difficult to put up with the
pain.* • *I can put up with the house being untidy, but I
hate it if it's not clean.* • *I don't know why she puts up
with him* (=is willing to accept his unpleasant
behaviour). • *They have a lot to put up with* (=They
have a lot of difficulties).

cut back/down on If you cut back/down on
something, you do less of it or use it in smaller
amounts: *The firm has cut back/down* **(on)**
wastage production/labour. ○ *The President wants
to cut back* **(on)** *defence spending by 10% next year.*
○ *I've decided to cut back on cigarettes/
alcohol/sweets.*

get down to *obj v adv prep* to start to direct your
efforts and attention to (esp. a piece of hard work)
• *I've got a lot of work to do but I can't seem to get
down to it.* [T] • *I must get down to sorting out that
pile of papers on my desk.* [+v-ing]

make up for *(obj) v adv prep* to take the place of
(something lost or damaged); to COMPENSATE
for something bad) with something good • *No
amount of money can make up for the death of a
child.* [T] • *This year's good harvest will make up for
last year's bad one.* [T] • *He bought me dinner to
make up for being so late the day before.* [+v-ing] • *I
went to university at the age of 45 and worked and
played very hard **making up for lost time*** (=using
and enjoying the experience as much as possible
because it hadn't happened sooner).

1 We never expected to *(encounter)* .... so many legal
problems.

2 We're behind schedule so we'll have to *(compensate)*
.... for lost time.

3 I find it difficult to *(tolerate)* .... his rude behaviour.

4 The new strategy didn't *(meet)* .... our expectations.

5 Let's *(start)* .... business straight away, shall we?

6 It would be good if we could *(abolish)* .... the excessive
red tape involved in setting up in business.

7 Times are hard and we've had to *(reduce)* ....spending.

C Now answer these questions.

1 What would you do with any money you might come into ?

2 What is the best way to put by money for a rainy day?

3 What kind of business would you put your money into?

4 What character traits would you expect in someone who was cut out
to set up and run a business?

5 During a recession, what do businesses try to cut down on?

6 Are there any regulations that should be done away with to make it
easier for a business to be successful?

3 Word building: *cost*

Read these dictionary extracts for *cost* and complete the sentences below with words from the box.

If an activity is **cost-effective** it is good value for the amount of money paid: *It wouldn't be cost effective to bring him over from New York just to give a seminar.* ○ *Improving energy efficiency is regarded as the most cost-effective way to reduce the enviromental impact of electricity generation.*

cost *obj* /£kɒst, $kɑːst/ *v* [T no passive] *past* cost • *"How much does this book cost (=What is the price of this book)?" "It costs £25."* • *It costs a lot to buy a house in this part of London.* • *I'd love to buy a Rolls-Royce but they cost an arm and a leg/a bomb/the earth/a packet/a small fortune (=they are very expensive).* • *The trip will cost you $1000.* [+two objects] • *The repairs to my car cost me a lot of money.* [+two objects] • *(infml)* **It'll/That'll cost you** *(=It will be very expensive)* *to have your roof mended.* • *Buying that second-hand car without having it checked by a mechanic first cost us dear (=we lost money because of it).* • LP **Two objects**

The **cost price** of an item is the price it cost to make, without a profit being added: *We were able to buy the furniture from a friend at cost (price).*

costs *obj* /£kɒst, $kɑːst/ *pl n* • Costs are the cost of something: *We need to cut our advertising costs.* ○ *The estimated costs of the building project are well over £1 million.* ○ *Workers fear the costs incurred in controlling pollution will cost them their jobs.* ○ *(law) The jury found the newspaper guilty of libelling the actress, and she was awarded damages and costs (=the cost of taking the matter to a law court).*

cost *obj* /£kɒst, $kɑːst/ *v* [T] *past* costed • To cost something is to calculate its future cost: *How carefully did you cost the materials for the new fence and gate?* ○ *Has your scheme been properly costed (out)?* [T/M]

It's not worth getting into an argument with Tim, as I learned **to my cost** *(=from my unpleasant experience of having done so).*

cost [SOMETHING GIVEN] /£kɒst, $kɑːst/ *n* [U] that which is given, needed or lost in order to obtain something

costing /£kɒstɪŋ, $kɑːstɪŋ/ *n* [C] • *We'll need accurate costings (=calculations of future cost) before we can agree to fund the scheme.*

cost•ly /£'kɒst-li, $'kɑːst-/ *adj* **-ier, -iest** • Costly means expensive: *Because the fee is calculated on a percentage basis, card holders pay more on costly items than they do on small purchases.* • *(disapproving) Our holiday in Australia proved (=was) very costly.* • *(disapproving) The project was subject to several costly delays/setbacks.* • LP **Expensive**

cost•ly /£'kɒst-li, $'kɑːst-/ *adj* **-ier, -iest** • *Building this bridge has already been too costly in terms of lives (=too many people have been killed while working on it).*

cost	costing	to our cost	costly
costed	costs	cost-effective	at cost price

1 A year ago, the network .... £500,000 to install.

2 We've .... the overall investment at £100,000.

3 Our .... gave us a net profit margin of 60 per cent on the sales price.

4 They had to pay a large fine plus .... for polluting a local river.

5 We sold off the surplus stock .... to get rid of it.

6 We learnt .... that our competitors had cornered the market.

7 Purchasing the equipment rather than just leasing it turned out to be a .... choice. It would have been a lot more .... to lease it.

4 Franchising

Many people who want to set up in business investigate the idea of franchising, that is creating your own business by purchasing the right to use another company's (the franchisor's) brand name, reputation and expertise.

On the recording you will hear a conversation between a potential franchisee, Trevor Franklin, and Wendy Rees, the franchise manager at a bank.

Franchise fee	training	£ 25,000
Fixtures/fittings		£
Computing		£
Display material		£
Premises		£
Working capital		£
Value added tax		£

As you listen, fill in the table below with the items of expenditure and the amount spent. The first one has been done for you.

5 Pronunciation: /sk/ /ʃ/ /tʃ/

Look at how these words are pronounced:

school   /skuːl/
champagne   /ʃæmˈpeɪn/
chair   /tʃeə/

Look at the words in the box below. Are the underlined parts pronounced /sk/, /ʃ/ or /tʃ/? Write the words in the correct column in the chart.

/sk/	/ʃ/	/tʃ/

bro<u>ch</u>ure	<u>ch</u>art	fran<u>ch</u>ise
<u>ch</u>allenge	<u>ch</u>eap	<u>sch</u>edule
<u>ch</u>arge	<u>ch</u>eck	<u>sch</u>eme

Check your answers with the recording. Then listen again and repeat the words.

▮6 Learning vocabulary

Many words that occur in texts are linked to other words. They may
mean roughly the same thing or be opposites or just belong to the
same general area of meaning. For example, look at the word
patterns in this passage:

> The average cost of a franchise is said to be £80,000, and when
> investigating the investment opportunities available to you, the initial
> capital outlay is very important. For established franchises most
> banks will lend you two-thirds of the money, so a few quick sums will
> tell you that if you have £30,000 cash available, you should be
> looking at businesses that cost up to £90,000. So, having done your
> arithmetic, you go off to select franchises in that price range.
> Perhaps you visit an exhibition or speak to some franchisors. Either
> way you will find a number of openings in your price bracket. Now
> you know what you can afford, all you have to do is decide which
> one to choose and how to raise the necessary funds.

When you read you can try to increase your word power by
recognising these connections for yourself.

Draw lines between the words in this passage that seem to you to be
connected.

> The existence of highly successful people who have made it on
> their own is the most powerful motivation for company executives to
> 'break out' – to purchase the companies they work for, buy into another
> firm or start a new business.
>
> But the spirit of enterprise needs someone to bankroll it: if
> company managers could afford to finance their break-outs themselves,
> they probably would not be working for other people in the first place.
> Banks are an obvious source of funds, but bank borrowing increases
> gearing and there is the danger that loans can be called in at any time.
> Venture capital, with the equity participation it involves, is a more
> secure basis for a fledgling business. Equity finance also spreads the
> risk, but at the cost of losing some control of the new venture.

14 Investment and finance

1 Related words: Financial terms

A Read through the newspaper extracts and underline all the words you think are associated with investment and finance. The first two in A have been done for you.

A

Blue Circle, Britain's biggest cement manufacturer, yesterday launched a £241.6m ($434.9m) <u>rights issue</u> to help pay for an <u>acquisition</u> to make it one of Europe's largest manufacturers of domestic heating products.

In the latest of a series of cross-border mergers involving European heating companies it announced it had acquired Compagnie Internationale du Chauffage for £124.9m.

Blue Circle proposes a one-for-five rights issue at 200p. Its shares rose 3p to 247p following the announcement of the issue.

B

BANCO ESPANOL de Crédito (Banesto) will place 26% of its non-banking interests on the market in mid-September. The $800m flotation will be underwritten by UBS Phillips & Drew.

C

Cathay Pacific has swung back into profit after record losses in the previous twelve months, prompting the airline to resume dividend payments.

Total turnover rose 21% to HK$17.91bn. This reflected both the 7% rise in traffic as well as a 10% increase in yields, generated mainly by higher-fare passengers.

B Match your underlined words to these definitions.

1 the parts into which the capital of a business is divided

2 the volume of business transacted in a given period

3 the amount produced from an investment (two possible words)

4 guaranteed

5 taken over

6 supply of shares for sale (two possible words)

7 floated (two possible words)

8 amalgamations

9 the opposite of profits

2 Word partners: Noun combinations

Some frequently-used words occur in many different combinations
and contexts.

A In each list only one noun can combine with each of the other
words. Choose the appropriate noun for each of the four lists.

capital	rate
market	share

1

a .... maker
.... share
a buyer's ....
futures ....
.... research

2

a .... of return
the exchange ....
the base ....
interest ....

3

working ....
a .... gain
venture ....
.... expenditure
to raise ....

4

a .... option scheme
a .... index
a .... issue

B How many word combinations can you make with *profit* and
asset(s)?

3 Guessing meaning from context

If you do not know the meaning of a word you read, you may be able
to discover its meaning from the words that surround it. Look at the
following extract.

> ## IBM SETS UP OFFSHOOTS TO RIVAL CHEAP PC CLONES
> IBM has created independent wholly-owned
> subsidiaries in the UK and Canada to sell
> low-cost personal computers that will com-
> pete with cheap look-alikes manufactured in
> the Far East.

We can see that *set up* and *created* are close in meaning, as are *offshoots*
and *wholly-owned subsidiaries*, *rival* and *compete with*, *cheap* and *low-
cost*, *clones* and *look-alikes*.

Read the following extracts and identify the words and expressions in each paragraph that are synonyms or near synonyms.

A

AIRLINES IN DRIVE TO ATTRACT BUSINESS PASSENGERS

Ever-growing numbers of people are flying, but Asian carriers are trying new advertising campaigns to lure more of them to the front of the plane. Although on the rise, sales of seats in business class compartments are not increasing fast enough to fill all the spaces available. Most of these aircraft were ordered before the economies of Europe, North America and Japan slowed down.

B

HEALTHY FINAL QUARTER CHECKS AKSO FALL

Akso, the Dutch chemicals group, succeeded in limiting the decline in net profit before extraordinary items to 2.7 per cent, thanks to a strong fourth quarter and better results in the US.

C

SHARE PRICE FALL FOR CHEMICAL GIANT AFTER POOR RESULTS

The share price of the Wellcome Foundation, the huge multinational pharmaceuticals and retail group, dropped 24p to 466p as the conglomerate reported disappointing pre-tax profits and sluggish growth. High hopes for Mesoplax, a new heart drug, failed to live up to expectations, and overseas operations, which account for 35% of turnover, also failed to reach their full potential in a lethargic world economy.

D

WESTCROSS SPURNS UNDERVALUED IPG OFFER

Westcross, the Irish engineering firm, yesterday flatly rejected the hostile £600m takeover bid from IPG. Sir Humphrey Rawstone urged shareholders to turn down IPG's proposal of 477p a share. "We have no doubt the bid does not reflect the true worth of our company," he said.

■4 Word partners: Compound nouns

Many words in finance and investment are noun combinations (for example, *takeover bid* in D above).

Match the words in box A with those in box B. If necessary, use a business dictionary and look up the headword from box A.

A	B
credit	assets
insider	bank
junk	bond
liquid	buyout
management	capital
merchant	issue
rights	line
venture	trading

5 Pronunciation: Letters which are not pronounced

Look at the word *underwritten*. The *w* is not pronounced. English has a number of words like this where one or more letters are silent.

Listen and underline the letters which are not pronounced.

climb	guarantee	receipt
debt	half	scheme
foreign	mortgage	wholly

Check your answers with the recording. Then listen again and repeat the words.

6 Raising funds

A Listen to the interview with Mary Cartwright, a financial expert in the City of London. What method of raising capital does she recommend for:

1 a young start-up company?

2 a multinational?

3 a small or medium-sized company?

B Listen again to the recording and note any advantages and disadvantages of each of the methods of raising capital mentioned.

Method	Advantages	Disadvantages

C How does *your* company, or a company you know, raise capital?

▌7 Related words: Financial ratios

Many of the terms used in finance involve the relationship between two sets of figures. Using a dictionary if necessary, match these words to their definitions.

debt-equity ratio	price-earnings ratio	working capital ratio
earnings per share	return on investment	

1 The .... is the after-tax profit of the firm divided by the number of shares in issue.

2 The .... is calculated by dividing the base profits of a group by the number of shares in issue.

3 The .... is current assets divided by current liabilities.

4 The .... is the relationship between a company's borrowings and its shareholders' funds.

5 The .... is the market price of a share divided by the current year's earnings per share.

▌8 Learning vocabulary

One of the ways in which the brain stores vocabulary is by making associations between words. These associations can be made by:

- synonyms
- opposites
- frequent combinations

- related meanings
- idiom

to underwrite a loan = to guarantee a loan
assets ≠ liabilities
high finance; to charge/bear interest; to raise funds; to drive a hard bargain
mergers and acquisitions
It's money down the drain; I'm broke; They haven't got a penny to their name

A What connections (in any order) can you make between the words in this grid?

bid	working	flotation	profit
earnings	net	gross	funds
equity	yield	launch	share
loss	takeover	raise	capital

B Make sentences to illustrate your associations. For example:

Bond and *debenture* are often used interchangeably, and are both a loan made by an investor to a company.

9 Win some, lose some!

Throw a dice. If you land on a square with information, decide if it increases or decreases the value of your investment. If it increases the value, move forward twice the score on your dice. If it decreases the value, go back twice the number on the dice.

60 **FINISH**	59	58 Failure of GATT talks leads to increased protectionism in world trade.	57	56
51 Your production plant relocates abroad. The foreign government provides a five-year tax haven and a low-cost loan to purchase the plant.	52	53 The government decides to nationalise major undertakings, including yours.	54	55
50	49	48	47 The Stock Exchange Commission accuses you of insider trading and attempting to rig commodity markets.	46
41	42 Panic selling on the Stock Exchange. The Dow Jones index falls by 30 points.	43	44	45
40	39 Political uncertainties threaten the stability of your export markets.	38 Computerised program trading gets out of control and gives rise to panic selling.	37	36 The government announces tax subsidies and price supports to stimulate investment in your industry.
31	32	33	34	35
30 The US government announces a record trade deficit.	29	28 Devaluation makes it cheaper for overseas buyers to purchase your goods.	27	26 The government has privatised several major state-owned industries including your own. Share prices have risen by 20% in just six months.
21 The government announces a 5% reduction in corporation tax.	22	23	24	25
20	19 Your Financial Controller has been embezzling funds. $20 million has gone missing (and your Financial Controller).	18	17	16
11 Unfavourable exchange rate leads to losses in your overseas subsidiary.	12	13	14	15 Massive World Bank loan to developing countries offers increased investment opportunities.
10	9 Windfall profit owing to currency fluctuations in your favour.	8	7	6
1 **START**	2 You complete a successful takeover bid of your major competitor. The value of your shares increases by 24%.	3	4	5 The government announces a decrease of 1% in the base lending rate.

15   Export payments

⬛1 Related words: Documentation

Export transactions involve considerable documentation.

A Read the following letter extract and underline all the documents mentioned.

> You should therefore receive the consignment within seven days of receipt of this letter. Please find enclosed your copy of the air waybill.
>
> The air waybill and the pro-forma invoice in triplicate have been forwarded together with the insurance certificate to the Banque Française du Commerce Extérieure for payment of your sight draft for FF47,985 (FOB Marseilles) in conformity with the irrevocable letter of credit.
>
> Please send the import licence and consular invoice to the customs authorities at the airport of destination.

B Now match the documents to their descriptions.

1   A bill of lading that covers both domestic and international flights transporting goods to a specified destination.

2   A document issued by a government authorising the importation of goods.

3   A document issued by a consulate describing the shipment and showing information such as the consignor, the consignee and the value of the goods.

4   A sample invoice to give a potential buyer information about prices and conditions of sale.

5   A means of payment via a bank which cannot be cancelled without the agreement of the party the payment is made to.

6   A document of payment which becomes payable on presentation to the debtor.

7   An attestation proving that the goods have been covered against loss or damage.

2 Abbreviations

Abbreviations are commonly used in international payments.

A Match the following abbreviations to the documents in Task 1.

B/L	AWB	L/C

B Do you know what the following commonly-used abbreviations mean?

@	COD	SWIFT
a/c	IOU	VAT
ASAP	NB	
B/E	RSVP	

C Put the correct abbreviation in each sentence. Choose from the list above.

1 .... is a world-wide telecommunications system used for inter-bank financial transactions.

2 If you want someone to answer quickly you could write 'Please reply ....'

3 At the bottom of a written invitation, to indicate that a reply is required, English uses the French abbreviation ....

4 On an invoice the price is quoted including and/or excluding ....

5 You might find the abbreviation .... on your bank statement.

6 This abbreviation is used before the unit price: for example, '25 rolls .... $150'.

7 If you read .... before a sentence you should take special notice.

8 To indicate that payment is to be made when the goods are delivered, ... is written.

9 The letters .... are an acknowledgement of a debt.

10 An .... is an order in writing which requires a person to pay someone a sum of money on demand.

▋3 Linking words: Sequencing (1)

A The illustration on the next page shows the steps in a documentary credit transaction between a British exporter and an overseas buyer (the importer). The twelve stages below are in the wrong order. Put them back into the correct order using the illustration to help you. (We have included four stages as a guide.)

A The issuing bank asks the UK bank to advise and/or confirm the credit line.

B The issuing bank releases the documents to the foreign buyer.

C The exporter despatches the goods to the overseas buyer.

D The exporter presents the shipping documents to the bank holding the credit, i.e. the UK advising/confirming bank.

E The overseas buyer is debited by the issuing bank in a previously agreed manner.

F The UK advising/confirming bank sends the letter of credit to the exporter.

G With the documents in their possession the overseas buyer takes delivery of the goods.

H A British exporter and an overseas buyer conclude a sales contract with payment to be arranged by documentary credit.

I The UK bank checks the documents, pays and/or accepts under the terms of the credit.

J The overseas buyer tells the issuing bank to provide a credit line in favour of the exporter.

K The issuing bank checks the documents and reimburses the UK bank.

L The UK advising/confirming bank forwards the documents to the issuing bank.

B Listen to a banker explaining the procedure. Did you find the right order?

▋4 Word partners: Verbs and nouns

Look back at the twelve stages. Which verbs are used with these nouns?

1 .... the documents

2 .... the goods

3 .... a contract

4 .... a payment

5 .... a credit line

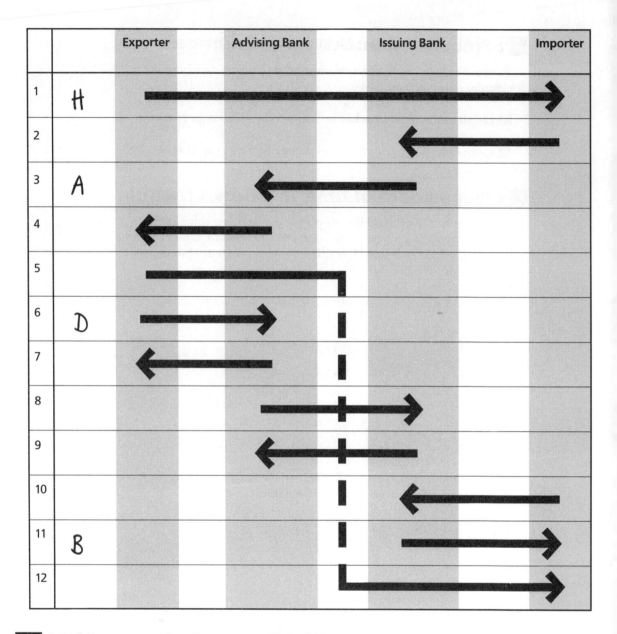

		Exporter	Advising Bank	Issuing Bank	Importer
1	H				
2					
3	A				
4					
5					
6	D				
7					
8					
9					
10					
11	B				
12					

▐5▌ Linking words: Sequencing (2)

Now combine the sentences in Task 3 so that they make one or more
acceptable paragraphs.

You should use *linking words* like those you heard on the recording:

first of all	then	and
secondly	next	finally
at this stage	after this	
at this point	when this has been done	

6 Pronunciation: Letters and numbers

To avoid certain confusion it is important to understand and say reference numbers clearly.

A Listen to the recording and take down the references you hear.

B If possible, write your own and dictate them to a colleague.

7 Prepositions of time: *in/on/by/at/within*

It is important to get paid for supplying goods or services but it is also important to get paid at the moment you want to. Late payments are not good for cash flow! For this reason, it is essential to master prepositions of time.

A Match the prepositional phrase in box A with its 'meaning' in box B.

A	B
in a week	after a specific period of time
on Friday 21 May	a particular moment
by the end of the month	before the end of a stated period of time
at 6 o'clock	a specific day or date
within two weeks	before or on a specific day, date or time

B Some prepositions are used with certain fixed expressions. Which preposition from the list is used in these expressions?

at	by	in	on

....	due course	....	request
....	this time next week/	....	arrival
	month/year	....	return of mail
....	the latest	....	advance
....	short notice	....	schedule
....	the earliest	....	delivery

C Complete these sentences using *in, on, by, at, within*.

1   Could you let me have the documents .... Friday week
    .... the latest?

2   The sales contract is due to be concluded .... ten days' time.

3   Payment will be made .... arrival of the goods.

4   You should receive payment .... the next two weeks.

5   It will be difficult to arrange payment .... such short notice.

6   We would be grateful if you would forward your cheque .... return of mail.

7   Payment is 10% .... advance, the remainder .... delivery.

8 Easily confused words: *in time / on time*

A Look at these two examples. What is the difference between the two expressions?

I arrived at the hotel just **in time** for a late supper.
The plane actually left **on time** so I wasn't late for the meeting.

B Complete these sentences with the correct expression.

1   It was a rush but we had everything ready .... for the Trade Fair.

2   We regret to inform you that, owing to a strike at one of our suppliers, we shall be unable to deliver ....

3   If possible, I'd like this meeting to finish ....

4   I don't know if I'll be able to complete the report .... for the committee meeting.

9 Learning vocabulary

'In my family we cut up paper into 2cm x 2cm cards. On each one we put a word we want to learn, then on another card we put the translation. Then we mix the cards and put them face-down. The first person turns over two cards and if it's a pair – an English word and its translation – they keep them and have another go. Otherwise the next person tries and so on until there are no cards left. The children enjoy it and words seem to stick.'

Bruno Fagandini (Italy)

16 Complaining and apologising

▮1 Related words: Consumer preferences

A Imagine you are buying a new car. Which of these factors would you consider *the most* important? Which is *the least* important? If possible, compare your answers with a colleague.

- a 10% discount
- a free gift
- a good part-exchange deal
- attractive credit financing
- friendly sales personnel
- reliable after-sales service
- two years' guarantee, parts and labour

B You have purchased a car phone and it is defective. You take it back to the store. Would you react positively or negatively if any of these was said?

1 We'll give you a full refund.

2 We'll exchange it for another one.

3 We'll give you a credit note.

4 Send it back to the manufacturer, it's still under their guarantee.

5 It was working when it left the store, you must have misused it in some way.

6 There's nothing we can do, the guarantee has expired.

7 We'll repair it for you free of charge.

8 We can't do anything if you've lost your receipt, we need proof of purchase.

" Well. That's more like it!"

2 Word building: Prefixes

A *prefix* is a word or syllable placed at the beginning of another word to change its meaning. For example: *ex-president* (a previous president); *pre-paid* (paid in advance).

A Look at these words. What do the prefixes mean?

disagreeable	imperfect	inadequate	unfair
dissatisfied	impolite	intolerable	unhelpful

B Match these words to those with similar meanings in the box above.

faulty	unpleasant	insufficient	unbearable
rude	unhappy	unjust	unsympathetic

C As a customer, when might you have to use each of the words from the boxes in A and B above?

3 Spelling: Suffixes *-ence/-ance*

It is often difficult to choose between the suffixes *-ence* and *-ance*.

Make nouns from these verbs. Be careful with the spelling.

accept	confer	occur	prefer
assist	insist	perform	refer
assure	maintain	persist	remit

4 Pronunciation: Word stress

A Say the verbs from Task 3. Is the stress on the first or the second syllable?

B Say the nouns from Task 3. Which syllable is normally stressed in nouns ending in *-ence* or *-ance*?

Which nouns in the list are very often pronounced with only two syllables? In this case, which syllable does the stress fall on?

C Listen to the recording and check your answers. Then listen again to the recording and repeat the words.

5 Related words: Making complaints

A Have you ever had to complain to a supplier or a retailer? In what circumstances?

- **Who did you complain to?**
- **How did you make the complaint?**
- **Were you *nervous, polite, firm* or *furious*?**
- **Did you obtain satisfaction?**

B Read the four extracts from faxes and decide which of the above adjectives could be used to describe each of them (you can use more than one).

A

29. May. 1996 8:10 BGI LTD No. 9849 P. 1/1

Further to our telephone conversation concerning the delivery of machine parts which should have arrived on 23 April, I must remind you that there is a penalty clause stipulating an indemnity of £2,000 for late delivery.

However, my accountant tells me that we have not yet received your remittance in respect of this penalty clause. I must therefore inform you that we are not prepared to settle your last statement.

I should also point out that your continued unreliability in the matter of deliveries has put the renewal of our contract in danger and I am currently talking with other suppliers who appear to be more willing to meet our requirements.

I await both your cheque and comments on this matter.

B

29. May. 1996 8:10   BGI LTD   No. 9849 P. 1/1

In all my years in business I can honestly say I have never seen return material in worse condition. Of the 74 rolls sent back, 30 were used more than 50%, and three rolls were not even our product. Everything that was shipped by us was in excellent saleable condition. In total contrast, the returned rolls are not usable or saleable, and this is entirely due to mishandling.

As I said on the phone, mishandling cannot be accepted as a valid reason for issuing credit. Thus, to avoid any legal or collection problems, I request immediate payment of the $4428.00 balance; owing on our invoice B18359. Hopefully, you will

C

29. May. 1996 8:10   BGI LTD   No. 9849 P. 1/1

As you know, we have purchased a substantial number of machines from your company in recent years and have been satisfied both with their performance and with the after-sales service offered.

Recently, however, we have had several reasons for complaint: on two occasions machines have broken down immediately following a routine service and, whereas in the past we could rely on your service engineer passing within 24 hours of a breakdown, over the last twelve months the delay has averaged three days.

This type of inefficiency unfortunately results in delays in our production schedules and cannot be allowed to continue. Unless, therefore, you

D

29.01.96 10:34 FAX 2514331   PRECISE LITHO   001

Please note that rapid deliveries to our plant are essential for us to maintain satisfactory stock levels and keep to production schedules.

Our latest order (WYT/54) arrived over two weeks late and we had to cut production by some 10%.

May I remind you that we cannot allow this situation to continue, as we cannot run the risk of losing orders through late deliveries. Unless there is a marked improvement and you are able to dispatch goods on the agreed dates, we will be

🔲 **C** Now listen to the telephone calls from customers complaining about various problems. As you listen, decide which fax was written by which caller.

D List any useful words or expressions from the letters under the following headings. The first four have been done for you:

Contracts	Payment	Delivery	Maintenance
renewal	indemnity	late	after-sales service

▌6 Easily confused words: *remind/remember*

A Compare the uses of *remind* and *remember* below:

I must **remind** you that there is a penalty clause.
May I **remind** you that we cannot allow this situation to continue?
We must **remember** to pay the $1000.
Did you **remember** to check the shipping documents?

What is the difference between them?

B When was the last time you had to remind your boss or a colleague to do something important? What did you say?

C What methods do you use to remember to do things?

▌7 Apologies

A How would you react to each of the faxes in Task 5? Would you contest what was written or would you apologise?

B This letter was sent in reply to one of the faxes. Which one?

We were extremely sorry to learn of the problems you have been having with our after-sales service department.

It is unfortunate that you have waited such a long time before informing us of the problems you have been having. However, we have now succeeded in resolving the problem of service delays after the recruitment and training of new personnel. In future, I will investigate any breakdowns following service visits personally.

Once again, I sincerely apologise for the difficulties you have encountered.

C Which words are used in the letter to express *regret*?

D This is part of a letter which was sent in reply to another one of the faxes. Which one?

> We are ¹ .... not to have been able to meet the delivery of machine parts for 23 April. This was due to a supply bottleneck which has now been ² .... The goods have now been dispatched and should reach you by Friday.
>
> Once again we ³ .... for any ⁴ .... and ⁵ .... you that you will receive ⁶ .... deliveries in future now that the situation has
> ⁷ ....

Use these words to complete it.

apologise	inconvenience	resolved	sorry
assure	prompt	returned to normal	

8 Learning vocabulary

How do you remember the spelling of a word? Compare your method with that of a colleague.

Which words do you find difficult to spell? Note them down, then check the spelling.

Look how one learner taught herself words ending in *-ence* and *-ance*.

'Well, I use my visual memory to help me. I picture a fence, because "fence" contains "-ence", then I picture a fence made up of all the verbs that take "-ence" as nouns: "conference", "reference", "insistence" and so on. Every time I come across a new one I just close my eyes and concentrate and add it to my fence.'

Akiko Hasegawa (Japan)

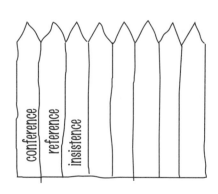

17 Information systems

1 A communications crossword

Try to find the words that correspond to the clues; the word printed vertically gives us a word that means more or less the same as *data*.

Clues (top to bottom):

- Use this to send your letters from one computer to another.
- A monitor or VDU.
- With this you can send a document anywhere in the world for the cost of a telephone call.
- If you dial this number the firm will pay the cost of your telephone enquiry.
- Keep a .... of everything, whether on paper or on disk.
- You link your computer to a telephone line by using a ....
- If you take someone else's phone call, ask the caller to leave a ....
- This kind of program enables you to make financial calculations.
- A kind of dossier.
- Computer programs on disk or CD-ROM.
- A firm's hardware is often linked together on a local area ....

▆2 Pronunciation: Stress in compound nouns

Look at the compound nouns below. Sometimes only one syllable is given prominence, sometimes two. For example:

■
keyboard

■   ■
filing system

 Listen and mark the stresses.

answerphone	phone call
display screen	photocopier
feedback	photocopy
laser printer	spreadsheet
message pad	training course

Now listen again to the recording and repeat the words.

▆3 Word grammar: Noun combinations

When two or more nouns are combined we:

- use *'s* for a person, a group of people or a time expression:
  Mrs Johnson's secretary
  the committee's opinion
  yesterday's meeting

- use *of* between the nouns, especially if they are inanimate or abstract:
  the history of telecommunications
  a breach of contract

- *of* is also used when the first noun focuses on a part or aspect of the second:
  the middle of the page
  a list of figures
  this type of problem

- use the first noun as an adjective. The last noun is the most important; the first noun tells us something about it and answers the question *What kind of ... ?*
  an instruction manual
  a warning system
  a car phone

Sometimes these nouns are joined by a hyphen (-) or make one word:
a ring-binder
a notepad
a handset
a keyboard

A Look at the following groups of nouns. Decide which of the following combinations are normal usage (✓) and which are wrong or sound strange (✗). For example:

the impact of technology (✓)
an information's revolution (✗)

1 telecommunications services

2 access points

3 data's transmission

4 area's networking

5 quantities of information

6 desktop computer

7 the computerisation information

8 the organisation database

9 a member of staff workstation

10 filing of systems

Now check your answers by reading the following passage.

The impact of technology is so great that we can justifiably talk of an information revolution. For example, the function of the mailroom to administer internal and external mail is being replaced by telecommunications services located at key access points. Such services include fax, telex, electronic data transmission, voice mail and e-mail. Thus, open area networking is bringing vast quantities of information to every manager's desktop computer. The computerisation of information enables the organisation's database to be kept constantly up to date and made available to any member of staff's work station from a mainframe (subject to security clearance or the use of a password). It is claimed that this makes centralised paper filing systems obsolete. This is not always the case, however, and Murphy's law ensures that if something can go wrong it will, and at the worst possible time.

B What other noun combinations are there in this passage?

◼4 Related words: Equipment

 Listen to some people talking about the equipment they use at work and decide which of the following they are referring to.

- a radiopager
- a mobile phone
- a car phone
- an electronic notepad
- an OCR scanner
- a multimedia videophone

Do you use any of these in your own situation?

◼5 Related words: Processing data

Look at the diagram entitled 'A systems model of information processing'. It shows how incoming information is dealt with and saved for future reference and onward distribution.

A Put these titles in the appropriate boxes (1-5) in the diagram.

FEEDBACK   STORAGE MEDIA   THE OUTPUT PHASE
INFORMATION PROCESSING   THE INPUT PHASE

A systems model of information processing

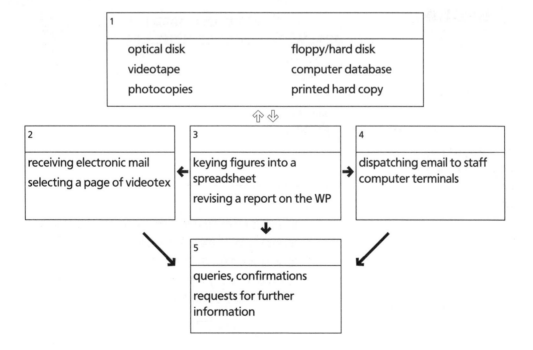

B Can you think of any other words and expressions to add under each heading?

C Put a tick in the box to indicate how often you do the following:

	Never	Sometimes	Often
make an audioconferenced telephone call	☐	☐	☐
select a page of videotex	☐	☐	☐
send or receive e-mail	☐	☐	☐
take part in a video conference	☐	☐	☐
use a database	☐	☐	☐
use a mobile phone	☐	☐	☐
use a videophone	☐	☐	☐

Which of these is/would be the most useful for you, and why?

6 Learning vocabulary

'I use a word processor a lot and constantly have to write and revise reports.
I find that the on-line Dictionary of Synonyms and Antonyms is very useful. For example, if I
want to use another word instead of 'number' then I click on the appropriate icon and get a
dialogue box with the meanings of the word:

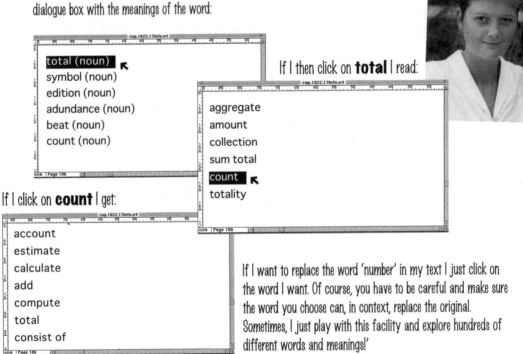

If I then click on **total** I read:

If I click on **count** I get:

If I want to replace the word 'number' in my text I just click on
the word I want. Of course, you have to be careful and make sure
the word you choose can, in context, replace the original.
Sometimes, I just play with this facility and explore hundreds of
different words and meanings!'

Danuta Wisniewska (Poland)

**Task: Start with the word *system* and think of words which are close in
meaning. Then select one of these words and think of other words
which are similar or related in some way. Choose one of these and
repeat the process.**

Answer key and tapescripts

1 Company organisation

1 Related words: Organisations and occupations

Individual answers
The category 'other' would include people who are self-employed or work for several clients.

2 Pronunciation: Syllable stress

▪ ▪▪ ▪ ▪
administrator

▪▪ ▪ ▪▪
business student

▪ ▪▪ ▪ ▪▪ ▪
computer programmer

▪▪ ▪▪ ▪ ▪▪
executive secretary

▪ ▪ ▪ ▪▪ ▪
financial consultant

▪▪ ▪ ▪ ▪▪ ▪
managing director

▪ ▪ ▪▪
receptionist

▪ ▪▪ ▪
Vice President

3 Easily confused words: *personal/personnel*

A *personal* means 'belonging to a particular person'; *personnel* means 'people employed in a company'

B ▪▪ ▪ ▪ ▪ ▪ ▪▪
personal; personnel

C **1** personal; **2** Personnel; **3** personnel; **4** personal

4 Talking about corporate structure

A 1 Corporate Planning; **2** Law, Patents and Insurance; **3** Public Relations; **4** Finance; **5** Research and Development; **6** Logistics; **7** Environmental Protection; **8** Human Resources; **9** Sales and Marketing; **10** Plant Administration

🔊 Tapescript

A: You work for one of the major European chemical multinationals. Could you tell us a little about how your company is organised?
B: Yes, well two years ago we moved over to an American-style structure with ... er ... what we call the Board of Management headed by the Company President, then ... er ... what we call the ... er ... Corporate Staff Division, which consists of ten divisions headed by ten Vice Presidents reporting directly to the Board of Management.
A: And what do each of these actually do?
B: As I said, there are ten Vice Presidents, each in charge of a division. These include Corporate Planning, Law, Patents and Insurance ... er ... I look after the patents section.
A: That's one division, Law, Patents and Insurance?
B: Yes ... Law, Patents and Insurance, then ... er ... oh, Public Relations and a few others.
A: Such as?
B: Such as Finance, R and D ...
A: Research and Development?
B: Yes, they're responsible for new product development ... and then there's Logistics, Environmental Protection ...
A: Environmental Protection? I'm surprised.
B: Yes, our company is a leader in the field.
A: Really?
B: Yes. We can trace our first actions back to 1901, and our clean air committee first met in 1913. We're very proud of that.
A: So you place a great deal of importance on environmental protection?
B: And at the highest levels, yes.
A: And what other divisions are there? Human Resources?
B: Yes, and ... er ... is that ten?
A: No, I don't think so.
B: No, where were we? There are ten ... er ... Finance, R and D, Logistics, Environmental Protection, Human Resources, Law, Patents and Insurance and er, oh Corporate Planning, of course, then ... er ... Sales and Marketing and Plant Administration.
A: And a Vice President takes care of each of these?
B: That's right.
A: And below that?
B: Well, below that there are the various departments that deal with the day-to-day running of the organisation, the sales function, invoicing, distribution and so on.
A: I see. Well, er ... thank you.

B 1 purchasing; 2 billing; 3 training;
4 market research; 5 audit; 6 distribution ;
7 plant

5 Word partners: Verbs and prepositions

be headed **by**; be responsible **for**; be in charge **of**;
report **to**; take care **of**; look **after**; deal **with**;
work **for**; consist of

6 Easily confused words: *subsidiary/agency/branch*

A 1 agency; 2 branch; 3 subsidiary

B 1 subsidiary; 2 agency; 3 subsidiary;
4 branch

2 The right person for the job

1 Related words: Applying for a job

A (for example) through newspaper
advertisements, employment agencies, personal
or business connections

B Suggested answers:

Title: *Sales Director*
Type of company: *major international
manufacturer of cash registers and point-of-sale
systems*
Responsibilities: *report directly to Chief Executive
Officer, expand Brazilian market share, play major
role in increasing sales effort in Latin America*
Type of person: *35/40, dynamic, hard-working,
motivated*
Skills: *proven track record in selling business
equipment*
Pay and benefits: *profit-related bonus, company car
and substantial salary*

Title: *South-East Asia Marketing Co-ordinator*
Type of company: *business and information
management consultancy*
Responsibilities: *advertising and public relations,
developing promotional literature, making
presentations, working with a network of national
marketing co-ordinators*
Type of person: *university graduate with a solid
background in marketing*
Skills: *solid background in marketing, fluency in at
least one Oriental language*
Pay and benefits: *not less than £40,000 equivalent +
profit-sharing and usual perks*

Title: *European Accountant*
Type of company: *fast-expanding public company
specialising in contract hire, equipment sales and
leasing*
Responsibilities: *report to the chief accountant,
responsible for a team of four involved with assets, cash
and company control – including preparation of
annual budgets and forecasts + advice on potential
acquisitions*
Type of person: *competent, disciplined*
Skills: *computer-literate*
Pay and benefits: *£40,000–£45,000 equivalent +
car, pension scheme, relocation assistance*

2 Synonyms: Job advertisements

1   are seeking/are looking for/are recruiting
2   calls for/requires
3   a proven track record/a background/
    experience
4   Duties include/Responsibilities include/
    The person will be responsible for
5   leading/major
6   play a key/play an important

3 Pronunciation: Word stress

Nouns	Verbs	Adjectives
˙present	˙present	˙present
	perfect˙	˙perfect
˙record	record˙	
˙permit	permit˙	
˙transfer	transfer˙	
re˙ject	re˙ject	

Nouns and adjectives tend to be stressed on the
first syllable, verbs on the second.

4 Word building: Adjective formation

A committed; confident; energetic;
enterprising; flexible; imaginative; independent;
powerful; promising; skilful; tactful; talented

B numerate; literate; articulate

5 Word building: Compound adjectives

1 far-reaching; 2 fast-thinking/working;
3 hard-working; 4 high-flying; 5 long-lasting;
6 well-educated

6 Pronunciation: Adjective endings

Words ending in *-ible* (and *-ate*) are stressed on the third-to-last syllable; words ending in *-able* are also stressed on the third-to-last syllable.

7 Personal skills

Possible answer:
This job calls for an articulate and numerate person with initiative. He or she should have a background in retail management.

8 Job specifications

A A man or woman with a sense of responsibility, independent, with initiative and energy, dynamic, hard-working, sensitive (but not too sensitive), tactful, articulate, with people skills. Someone with experience as a team leader and in the retail trade, preferably with a degree in business. Fluent in English, French and at least one other language.

B *Individual answers*

▱ Tapescript

A: What about this post of Retail Manager we're going to advertise, John? What kind of person are we looking for?
B: Well, it's a job which requires a sense of responsibility ... and ... er ... independence, since the person selected will be running, at the start at any rate, will be running ten stores with about 100 staff.
A: And with the possibility of expanding to 15 stores and 150 staff.
B: Right. So there's plenty of scope for initiative and energy ... and, of course, hard work.
A: So at the moment we're looking for someone who's responsible, independent, dynamic, hard-working and has initiative ...
B: That's it. But also someone able to deal with upwards of a 100 or a 150 staff.
A: So someone sensitive, tactful and articulate.
B: Yes, but not *too* sensitive: he is still the boss.
A: Wait a minute, why does it have to be a man?
B: Sorry, he or she ... Yes, OK, so this is very much a job requiring people skills, so I'd personally like to see someone who's had quite a lot of experience as a team leader.
A: OK. Now, this is a retail job – and a pretty high-powered one at that – so I guess we want someone with a certain amount of retail experience.
B: Absolutely, and not just a certain amount, either. Whoever we choose should have a substantial amount of experience in retailing – perhaps ... um ... in terms of organising a franchising operation or something like that – and also experience as a retail manager.
A: Just a minute, what do you mean by 'a substantial amount'? Five, ten, 20 years?
B: Well, I think he – sorry, he or she – would have to be at least 30.
A: Yes, OK. So we'll put in the advertisement 'proven track record as a retail manager'. How about education?
B: Well, it would be nice to have someone well-educated – with a good degree in business, say – but it's not essential. What is essential, though, is the personal skills and the right experience ... oh, and the language.
A: Yes, I was coming to that. We're an American company based in France, so presumably the person recruited should be fluent in both English and French.
B: Yeah, that's absolutely essential, and with at least one other language, since a lot of the employees will probably be from other countries.

9 Learning vocabulary

Nouns	Verbs	Adjectives
subsidy	subsidise	subsidised
benefit	*benefit*	beneficial
proof	prove	proven
success	succeed	*successful*
promotion	*promote*	promotional
expansion	expand	expanding
promise	*promise*	promising
pleasure	please	*pleasant/ pleasurable/ pleasing*
innovation	*innovate*	innovative

3 Pay and perks

1 Priorities

Individual answers

2 Easily confused words: salary/wage(s), etc.

A **1** earned income; **2** unearned income; **3** royalties; **4** wages; **5** fringe benefits
NB: The word *famil.* in the dictionary entry is an abbreviation of 'familiar'. This means a relatively informal term.

B **1** (unearned) income (NB: not *dividends*; dividends are *received*, not *earned*)
2 perks/fringe benefits; **3** fees; **4** wage(s);
5 revenue; **6** earnings/income

C *Individual answers*

3 Related words: Pay and perks

A 1 salary; 2 wages; 3 company car;
4 expense account; 5 low-interest loan;
6 bonus; 7 commission; 8 overtime;
9 luncheon vouchers; 10 private medical
insurance; 11 share option scheme

NB: A share option scheme could also
be considered a fringe benefit.

B *Individual answers*

C a factory worker: wages; overtime; bonuses

a sales representative: salary; commission;
company car; expense account

a senior manager: salary; company car; expense
account; share option scheme; private medical
insurance

an executive secretary: salary, luncheon vouchers

4 Pronunciation: Linking

A Normally such linking occurs when there is a
pronounced consonant at the end of the first word,
and a *pronounced* vowel at the beginning of the
second.

B medical‿insurance
share‿income‿and‿dividends
unearned‿income
head‿office
per‿annum

(Note how there is linking with *and dividends*
where the final sound of the first word is the
same as the first sound of the second.)

5 Performance-related pay

A 1 Performance-related pay is a wage or salary
paid (or usually increased) according to how well
you are doing your job.
2   Appraisal is a system (usually in the form of
an interview with your head of department)
where you discuss how well you have done your
job and met your objectives over a particular
time period.

B 1 Possible answers:
Advantages
It may motivate employees.
It gives the company the opportunity to reward
good employees.
Disadvantages
It may decrease co-operation among colleagues
by making them compete for limited funds.
It may be abused because bosses may only look at
what hasn't worked, and use this as an excuse not
to increase salaries.
Where there is a personality problem between an

employee and his/her boss, this may influence
the boss's decision.

2   It should apply to all employees whose
individual performance can clearly be separated
from their colleagues' work.
3   It should definitely be someone in a more
senior position, but in conjunction with a
colleague; and there should be an effective
appeals procedure.
4   There would need to be a period of
consultation and explanation of, say, three
to six months, followed by one or two years
(depending on the size of the department and
the number of problems revealed at
the consultation stage) for it to come into
operation.
5   Generally against, because of the possible
abuses.
6   Solution (b) seems the most reasonable,
in the first instance.
7   Appraisers need to be trained and there
should be an appeals procedure.

C The scheme applies to *all* employees, but only
those 'who've worked hard and contributed
something to the company's success' receive
extra money.

Each section head is responsible for the
appraisals of their staff.

In this company, introducing the scheme is
obviously going to take longer than two years,
since it started last year, will be extended to
senior managers next year, and will eventually be
extended to everyone. She mentions three years.

She expects staff – especially younger staff – to
be in favour.

🔊 Tapescript

A: Mrs Jackson, you are the senior partner in
a firm of chartered accountants which recently
decided to introduce performance-related pay
from the very top – partners like yourself – down
to the very bottom – clerical staff, trainees and
so on. Can you tell me why you thought this
was necessary?
B: Yes, well, previously I used to have 10% of
the profits to er distribute among the partners
more or less at my discretion.
A: As *you* wanted to? It was entirely your choice?
B: Yes ... er ... we've recently increased this
amount to 25%, but this 25% is now distributed
according to performance.
A: So whereas in the past *every* partner got his or
her share of the bonus, now it's only those who
deserve it, who've worked hard and contributed
something to the company's success?
B: That's the idea, yes, and ... er ... we're
expanding that system that idea down bit by bit.
Next year, for example, it'll extend to managers

and so on but it's not the kind of thing you can introduce all at once – er ... you have to ... it takes time and you have to educate people and train them and convince them – though generally, I think, people welcome the idea of reward matching contribution, of ... er ... earnings being related to how much you have contributed to the success of the business. And I think people, especially younger people, are keen to learn about their progress, review their successes and analyse their failures.

A: And what are the advantages for the firm?

B: For the firm it's a good way of defining goals and perhaps also identifying problems before they occur and become major failures or causes for dismissal. So yes, I think that there has ... there's been a strong body of support for the system, the ... er ... principle of the system.

A: So how long will it take before the whole system is in operation?

B: Well, you can't launch a scheme like this in one year. As I said, it requires education and training and these things take time so ... well ... we won't get it right first time so there will have to be modifications so I see this as a three-year programme with another ... it'll need another two years to become habit.

A: Who actually does the appraisals?

B: Basically each section head is responsible for the employees in his or her section and has to assess their performance for the year.

A: OK, but how do *they* appraise? How are they able to judge an employee's success or otherwise?

B: Well, they need training too. The danger is that judgements can be subjective and so we've established fixed criteria which are in relation to the ... er ... firm's objectives. The system would break down if promotion were made whether or not an individual had a poor appraisal. And we try to make sure that we don't allow a high rating in one area to influence ratings in others.

A: How *do* you rate, in fact?

B: We've now drawn up a set of criteria – a grid – and each employee is graded out of five on each ... er ... point on the grid and then given an ... an overall score out of five – the average if you like.

A: And if someone gets a low average?

B: Then they know in which areas they're performing badly and they have an appraisal meeting to work out a plan to improve performance and this plan has to be in operation within three months. I think it's a good scheme but it needs a lot of commitment and it does also unfortunately tend to produce rather a lot of bureaucracy.

6 Easily confused words: *raise/rise*

A *raise* is transitive; *rise* is intransitive

B **1** rose; **2** rise; **3** raised; **4** risen

C *Individual answers*

7 Related words: Conditions of employment

1 appointment; **2** remuneration package;
3 starting salary; **4** medical insurance;
5 performance-related bonus; **6** scales;
7 under review; **8** rise; **9** paid leave;
10 terms and conditions

8 Learning vocabulary

A possible network for *taxation*, containing some key terminology such as *corporation tax*, *capital gains*, *deductions*, and so on:

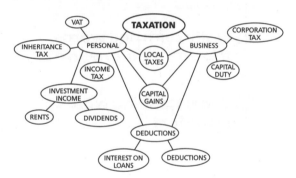

4 Travel

1 Reasons for travelling

A *Individual answers*

B **1** to sit on committees/once a week on average
2 visiting local agents to keep them up to date/once a month
3 to hold seminars/a lot of the time
4 to check on progress on sites and liaise with local sub-contractors/ten or more days a month

🔊 Tapescript

1 I travel about once a week on average. I'm based in Hong Kong, but I have to go to Taipei – our Head Office is there – to sit on various committees, particularly the Finance Committee, so I just jump on the plane in the morning and get back late evening, if all goes well. Sometimes I stay two or even three days if there's a problem that needs sorting out.

2 I work in the export department and I have to

go abroad much more often than I would like to. In fact, I hate travelling, living out of a suitcase, being cut off from wife and family.

I used to think it was fun but not now – I suppose I'm just getting old. Anyway, I travel abroad about once a month. I have to spend a few days with our local agents in places like Thailand, Japan, Italy, Brazil, Saudi Arabia just to make sure that they're kept up-to-date with what's happening in London.

3 I'm a freelance management training consultant and hold seminars on all sorts of subjects likely to interest executives in top management positions. So I spend a lot of the time travelling around the country in order to give presentations or speak at conferences.

4 We are a construction company specialising in delivering turnkey plants in developing countries. So I regularly go out to the sites to see what kind of progress is being made and liaise with local sub-contractors. I suppose that in any one month I spend at least ten days abroad, perhaps more.

2 Easily confused words: trip/travel/journey/tour

1 tour; **2** trip; **3** travel; **4** journey

3 Understanding words in context

Possible answers:
venue = place where the conference takes place
fees = the price
reception = introductory party
delegates = people attending the conference
refreshments = something to eat and drink
refund = money paid back
proceedings = an account of what happened at the conference
discounted = reduced in price

4 Pronunciation: Words ending in -ion

A

Nouns	Verbs
accommodation	accommodate
administration	*administer*
application	apply
cancellation	cancel
confirmation	*confirm*
delegation	*delegate*
notification	notify
option	opt for
presentation	*present*
reception	*receive*
registration	*register*

B The stress is on the syllable before the *-ion*.

accommodation   notification
administration   option
application   presentation
cancellation   reception
confirmation   registration
delegation

5 Related words: Transportation

A

Air	Road	Rail
baggage reclaim	(bus) fare	connection
boarding card	driving licence	fare
check-in desk	driver's license	platform
connection	fare (taxi)	restaurant car
departure lounge	self-drive	return ticket
fare	shuttle (bus)	shuttle
flight attendant	unlimited	track
gate	mileage	
return ticket		
shuttle		
stopover		
transfer		

B

cabin/flight attendant:
Can I get you anything else?
Red or white?

car rental clerk:
Have you a clean driving licence?
Do you want full collision protection?

conference receptionist:
It's in the main lecture theatre.

customs officer:
What is the purpose of your visit?

hotel receptionist:
I'm afraid there's no one of that name. Are you sure a reservation was made?

mechanic:
It was overheating because the fan belt was loose. Shall I check the oil?

police officer:
You can't park here.

taxi driver:
Shall I put it in the boot?

travel agent:
The 4.45 doesn't stop at Coventry.

waiter:
Are you ready to order now?
Can I get you anything else?
Red or white?
Sorry, it's off.

6 Synonyms: British and American English

(BrE = AmE)

lift = elevator
flat = apartment
autumn = fall
bill = check
driving licence = driver's license
garden = yard
ground floor = first floor
motorway = freeway
pavement = sidewalk
petrol = gas
puncture = flat
timetable = schedule
toilet = rest room
boot = trunk
tube (underground) = subway

5 Welcoming visitors

1 Related words: Appointments

1 make (or arrange); **2** keep, early; **3** postpone;
4 confirm; **5** fix (or arrange); **6** cancel;
7 punctual, late; **8** time;

2 Customs

Possible answers for the UK:

A It is usual practice to shake hands with both men and women the first time you meet them or if you meet them infrequently.

First names are commonly used among people at the same level in the hierarchy and even with superiors. Much depends on the culture of the organisation and the length of time people have been together.

It is important to be punctual for an appointment.

Working hours are relatively flexible with many employees able to choose the times at which they come to work as long as they are present for the required number. As you move up the hierarchy working hours tend to become longer as more individual commitment is expected.

Tipping in hotels and restaurants is common – calculate 10–15% of the bill. Taxi drivers also expect to be tipped.

Drinking is not encouraged by some organisations during the day. For example, at a conference, alcohol may not be served at lunch time.

Smoking is less common than it was. There may be a special smoking area. Do not forget to ask colleagues 'Do you mind if I smoke?'

Religion is not part of business life.

B You do not have to be absolutely punctual and you should definitely not be early. People often say things like 'Come at 8 for 8.30', which means about 8.25–8.45! It is common to bring a bunch of flowers for the hostess or a box of chocolates. A colleague or friend could bring a bottle of wine. However, if it is an upmarket business event, bringing a bottle of wine would not be appropriate.

C *Individual answers*

3 Related words: Wining and dining

A brunch = breakfast + lunch combined; it takes place late morning or early afternoon

lunch = a meal sometime between midday and three o'clock

tea = a light meal; late afternoon

the happy hour = the first hour when the bars open and drinks are usually sold cheaper (especially in the USA)

dinner = a meal sometime in the evening; sometimes also used for a meal at midday

supper = a meal in the evening

B *entrée* in the United States = main course
entrée in Great Britain = starter

C Probable order: appetisers; starters; main courses; side dishes; desserts; beverages

D Possible dialogue:
- Good evening, we booked a table for two in the name of Watson.
- Yes, of course, just follow me, please. (...)
- Have you chosen?
- No, not yet. Er, could you tell me what mixed grill is, please?
- Yes, it's a selection of different grilled or fried meats – kidneys, ham and so on – with black pudding.
- Oh, I see.
- Would you like to order?
- Yes, I'd like the T-bone steak, please. What would you like, Alexandros?
- I'd like the moussaka, please.
- Could we have the wine list?
- Of course, sir. (...)
- I enjoyed that.
- Yes, it was delicious.
- I'll pay.
- No, no, let me, I insist.
- OK, that's very kind of you.

– That's all right.
– Waiter, could we have the bill, please?
– Of course, sir.
– Er, is service included?
– Yes, sir.
  (...)
– Here you are, sir.
– Thank you. Er, do you accept American Express?

E The order is:
We booked a table for .... in the name of ....
Just follow me, please.
Have you chosen?
Could you tell me what .... is, please?
Would you like to order?
What would you like?
I'd like .... , please.
Could we have the wine list?
I'll pay.
Could we have the bill, please?
I insist.

We do not hear 'Do you accept American Express?' and 'Is service included?'

Note that we use the expression 'Say when' when we are pouring a drink into someone's glass and want the person to tell us when to stop.

F He says 'Could you tell me what a prawn cocktail is?'

G *Individual answers*

Tapescript

Waiter:	Good evening.
Joanna:	Good evening, we booked a table for two in the name of Williams.
Waiter:	Ah yes, just follow me, please.
Pierre:	Nice place.
Joanna:	Yes, we always bring our French customers here: it's the only place they like the food. ... Have you chosen?
Pierre:	For the main course, yes, I'd like the T-bone steak, please. But could you tell me what a prawn cocktail is?
Joanna:	Oh yes, well it's – er – a kind of mixture of prawns – you know, small pink shellfish – and, er, lettuce in a mayonnaise sauce.
Pierre:	I see ... Well, what do you recommend?
Joanna:	The steak's very good here.
Waiter:	Would you like to order now?
Joanna:	Yes, er, what would you like, Pierre?
Pierre:	er, the T-bone steak and er, the ... er ... I think I'll have the *pâté* to start with.
Waiter:	Yes, sir. And how would you like your steak?
Pierre:	Rare, please.
Waiter:	And you, madam?
Joanna:	I'd like a fruit juice to start and ... er ... then, er, a T-bone steak as well, please. But well done. And ... er ... could we have the wine list? I'm sure you'd like some wine, Pierre.
Pierre:	Oh, yes.
Waiter:	Of course, madam.
	(...)
Joanna:	Another drop of wine?
Pierre:	Please.
Joanna:	Say when.
Pierre:	That's fine, thanks.
Joanna:	Cheers; here's to good business relations.
Pierre:	Cheers, yes.
Joanna:	Coffee?
Pierre:	Er, no, I don't think so, or I'll have trouble sleeping tonight.
Joanna:	Right, then, I'll pay. Excuse me! Could we have the bill, please?
Pierre:	No, you paid in France. Let me, it'll go on expenses.
Joanna:	But ...
Pierre:	No, no, really, I insist.
Joanna:	OK, then; thanks a lot.
Pierre:	You're welcome.

4 Easily confused words: *pay/pay for*

pay: the bill/a hotel receptionist/a taxi driver/ a waiter
pay for: breakages/the drinks/a phone call/ room service/a taxi ride/a train ticket

5 Related words: Accommodation

A *Individual answers*

B In the event of fire ...
In all parts of the hotel (a good hotel should show fire notices everywhere!)

Hello, I've booked a room under the name of ...
at Reception

I'd be grateful if you could send me up ...
In a bedroom

Would you just sign here, please?
In the dining room/at Reception/in the bar/ in a bedroom (with room service)

Could you add it to my bill, please?
In the dining room/at Reception/in the bar/ in a bedroom (with room service)

Do you take American Express?
In the dining room/at Reception/in the bar

Could I be woken up at seven o'clock, please?

At Reception/in a bedroom

Could I leave these in the hotel safe?
At Reception

Could you bring the wine list?
In the dining room

I'm afraid the trout is off.
In the dining room

Draught or bottled?
In the dining room/in the bar

Guests must vacate the room by 11 a.m.
In a bedroom

6 Word grammar: Multi-word verbs

1 It turned out to be a disaster.
2 They set off at about five o'clock.
3 She dropped him off outside the terminal.
4 The flight had taken off.
5 He checked in for the next flight.
6 He kept trying to ring them up in Prague but couldn't get through.
7 No one picked him up at the airport.
8 He took a taxi and turned up at their offices.
9 The meeting had been called off.
10 One of his contacts showed him round and took him out to a restaurant.
11 The same person put him up for the night.
12 They got on very well together.

▣ Tapescript

A: Hi, Naseem, how was your trip to the Czech Republic?
B: Oh, that!
A: I thought you wanted to go?
B: I did, but it turned out to be a disaster.
A: Why was that?
B: Well, it was last Tuesday. My wife and I set off for the airport really early, about five o'clock, and of course there just had to be an accident on the motorway and a three-mile tailback. Anyway, we finally got there and she dropped me off outside the terminal but of course by that time my flight had already taken off and so I had to check in for the next flight which wasn't until a couple of hours later. I had nothing very much to do except read a paper and keep trying to ring them up in Prague to say I would be late but for some reason I couldn't get through. Anyway, I got the next plane and of course there was no one to pick me up at the airport but I took a taxi hoping I'd be still able to take part in some of the discussions, and I turned up at their offices much to their surprise.
A: Surprise? Why would they be surprised?
B: That's the point. The meeting had been called off! Apparently I'd been sent a fax but it had never reached me.

A: So what did you do then?
B: Well I was very lucky. One of my contacts showed me round their premises and kindly offered to put me up for the night and in fact took me out to a very nice restaurant and we got on very well together.
A: So it wasn't a *total* disaster.
B: No, I suppose not. And as the next meeting's here I'll make sure their delegation gets the red carpet treatment.

7 Pronunciation: Stress in multi-word verbs

If the verb and particle are separated, the stress is on the particle.
If the verb and the particle are not separated, there is equal stress.

6 Advertising

1 Word partners: compound nouns

Ⓐ 1 brand; 2 advertising; 3 market; 4 sales

Ⓑ 1 market leader; 2 advertising expenditure; 3 brand image; 4 sales promotion

2 Related words: Advertising media

Ⓐ Inside the home: direct mail, magazines, newspapers, radio, television
Outside the home: cinema, hoardings, point-of-sale, posters, sponsorship

Ⓑ 1 cinema; 2 direct mail; 3 hoardings; 4 sponsorship; 5 magazines; 6 point-of-sale

3 Related words: Printed material

1 insert; 2 leaflet; 3 catalogue; 4 voucher; 5 flyer

4 Word partners: Compound adjectives

Ⓐ 1 economy-size; 2 multi-purpose; 3 precision-built; 4 relief-giving; 5 space-saving; 6 trouble-free; 7 ultra-modern; 8 user-friendly

B These answers are to some extent subjective, but we feel these are the most usual collocations.

a lamp: 7
industrial detergent: 1, 2
software: 2, 6, 8
a sports car: 3, 6, 7
office furniture: 2, 5, 7
washing powder: 1
medicine: 4

C *Individual answers*

5 Easily confused words: make/brand/trademark

A Makes: Volvo, Miele, Yamaha: i.e. the name of the producer.
Brands: Marlborough, Nescafé, Persil: i.e. the name of the product.

B 1 Shell; 2 McDonald's; 3 Apple; 4 Mercedes

6 Pronunciation: Vowel sounds

A /əʊ/: poster; notice; radio; slogan
/aʊ/: outlet; account; sound; voucher
/ɔɪ/: point-of-sale; employer; loyalty
Other words heard: forecast, hoarding, offer, product

7 Launching a new product

1 objectives; 2 campaign; 3 media; 4 drive;
5 budget considerations; 6 background;
7 project; 8 purchasing decisions;
9 market research; 10 average household;
11 quality product; 12 up-market; 13 appeal;
14 gain; 15 launch; 16 foothold; 17 fierce;
18 prime time rates; 19 expenditure;
20 share of sales on the market; 21 launch

🔲 Tapescript

Makin: Right, let's get this meeting under way, shall we? We're here today to discuss the overall objectives of the campaign for the new GARDENFRESH line of ready-to-eat salad dishes. In particular we will need to talk about the media we'll be using, how long the advertising drive will last, and of course budget considerations. First of all, Terence, could you start the ball rolling by filling in Mark and Pamela on some of the background to the project?
Bride: Sure. Well, as you know the convenience food market is very complex and fast-moving with different fashions influencing purchasing decisions – health, sport, the environment and that sort of thing. We've done a great deal of market research and I think we've a pretty good

idea of what the average household is now looking for. First, it has to look attractive. Second, it has to be easy to make. Third, it has to taste good. Fourthly, and this is related to my third point, people are prepared to spend quite a lot more on a real quality product.
Brown: So you think this will be quite an up-market product.
Bride: Yes.
Brown: Does it appeal to both men and women?
Makin: Well, probably more to women but there are a lot of men, particularly single men, who do quite a lot of meal preparation.
Brown: Uh huh, I get the picture. So what are your overall campaign objectives?
Makin: We would hope to gain at least 15% of the Irish market and 5% of the British market within six months of launch. Subsequently, in year two we would hope to move into mainland Europe and gain a foothold there.
Saunders: That would be quite a challenge given the fierce competition. Still, it's not the first time we've handled such an account. But we couldn't deal with a campaign outside Britain.
Makin: No, quite, we understand that. Perhaps we could look at the second item on the agenda? Mark, do you have any ideas on this?
Brown: Yes, I definitely feel we need a full TV campaign but unfortunately prime time rates have been rising rapidly recently, so financing is going to be an important consideration – I mean, it always is but you may have to spend proportionately more than you originally wanted to.
Makin: Well, if we work on the principle that the share of expenditure on advertising for a given product should be roughly equivalent to its share of sales on the market I think we can aim at about 5% for Britain and 15% for Ireland.
Bride: Yes, I agree, but this is a launch so we will probably have to put more money in.
Saunders: We've begun to talk about item three …

8 Your brief
Individual answers

7 Getting things done

1 How do you organise your work?
Individual answers

2 Easily confused words: efficient/effective

1 efficient; 2 effective; 3 effective; 4 efficient

❸ Priorities

Individual answers

❹ Word grammar: Verb patterns

A verb + direct object + *to* + verb: get/help/instruct/offer/persuade/request/remind/require

verb + direct object + verb: have/help/make
(Note that *help* goes into both categories.)

B *Individual answers*

❺ Word partners: Verbs and nouns, compound nouns

A start from scratch; reach a target/a decision; implement a decision; troubleshoot a problem; meet a target/a deadline; deal with a problem; monitor progress; carry out a decision; handle a problem

B **1** end result; **2** progress report; **3** time scale; **4** trial run; **5** check list; **6** contingency plan; **7** target date

❻ Listening

A

1 Copywriter produces final copy
2 Brief art department
3 Art department produces final layouts
4 Secretary checks catalogue proofs
5 Catalogue is printed
6 Equipment is delivered

B

1 to plan; **2** plan of action ... time scale; **3** advance notice; **4** briefs; **5** deadline; **6** progress ... deals with ... crop up; **7** smoothly; **8** schedule; **9** the last minute

🔲 Tapescript

A: One of the things I have to do is to look after a stand at exhibitions and trade fairs and I'm responsible for seeing that everything is co-ordinated properly and goes to plan.
B: And what does that involve?
A: Well, first of all we spend four to five days discussing all the requirements and also how much money we can spend and once a decision has been made on what we need and the budget then I start to draw up a plan of action and set myself a time scale for doing things. Generally, I would say it takes about 12 to 13 weeks to get everything organised from start to finish. So I draw up a little chart of all the tasks that need to be done and put them into some sort of sequence. Then I make enquiries with all the people who will be involved and try to work out how long each stage will take. So, for example, I

know that they need 90 days' advance notice to book the stand.
B: 90 days?
A: That's right. But in fact I don't need to book the stand straight away. The first thing I do is talk to the copywriter of the catalogue we produce and brief her on what should go into it. Then it will normally take her 20 days to write all the text and produce the copy.
B: I see.
A: At this stage I also brief the art department and the design team will do specimen layouts. As soon as they have the final copy they produce *final* layouts. I set them a deadline of 25 days. On the whole they're very good, they keep to the time scale but I monitor progress and deal with any problems that might crop up.
B: What sort of problems?
A: Well, normally everything goes smoothly but there could be a software problem or possibly someone having to be transferred to another assignment or someone off sick.
B: Uh huh.
A: If they *are* running behind schedule I gently remind them that we need to respect the dates. When the layouts are ready the artwork is commissioned, and at the same time, we do any necessary photography. I try to persuade colleagues to pose for photographs because an agency is expensive. And it's round about now that I get people to start work on designing the stand, because that can take three weeks. Then I get my secretary to make any corrections to the catalogue proofs and she does that within the next ten days. While she's doing this I order any equipment that we will need for the stand because the supplier will need 30 days' advance notice for it to be delivered. At the same time the disks are sent to the printer's and the printing is done over the next 28 days, and if all goes well comes back in time for us to ship everything off if the trade fair is being held abroad. And if everything has gone to plan, this coincides with the delivery of the equipment I've ordered and it goes off together with the catalogues.
B: That sounds very complicated but you seem to be extremely efficient.
A: Well, I don't like leaving things to the last minute – you can't afford to because if you did, nothing would be done on time and the whole thing would be chaos, wouldn't it?

7 Pronunciation: Consonants

🔊 Tapescript

A: I've checked her figures.
B: It's been a hectic week, it's been all systems go.
A: It's difficult to estimate the length of time needed.
B: You have to calculate the risks.
A: I've been rushed off my feet and I'm beginning to feel I can't cope.
B: We didn't have enough money so the plan's been shelved for the time being.
A: We're a bit stretched this week – three people in our department are on sick leave.
B: I made a short list of tasks to get through.

8 Learning vocabulary

For example:
Adjectives followed by *of*: afraid; aware; capable; certain; full; proud; short; unsure; worthy

Verbs followed by *of*: approve; complain; disapprove; dispose; hear; know; think

Adjectives followed by *with*: annoyed; bored; compatible; fed up; involved; satisfied; unfamiliar

Verbs followed by *with*: deal; cope

8 Meetings

1 Reasons for meetings

A Possible answers:
to communicate *ideas/opinions*
to make *plans*
to plan *the future/the budget*
to pool *ideas*
to settle *differences*
to solve *problems*

B **1** They'll have to reconsider it.
2 We'll have to redraft it.
3 We'll have to reschedule it.
4 We'll have to reorder some.
5 You'll have to reread them.

NB: These verbs can also be written with a hyphen (re-schedule, re-consider).

2 Types of meetings

board meeting (the meeting of the company directors)

steering committee (a committee which is responsible for implementing a plan)

sub-committee (a part of a larger committee with a special responsibility)

think-tank (a group of experts who meet to brainstorm problems)

3 Organisation of meetings

Individual answers

4 Word partners: Verb and noun combinations

adjourn the discussion/a meeting
approve the minutes
draw up an agenda
hold/call a meeting
implement a decision
put something to the vote
raise an objection
record a decision
second the proposal
set a time limit
table a motion
write up the minutes

5 Setting an agenda

Possible answers:
Apologies for absence and minutes of the previous meeting are likely to come first. Matters arising usually refers to points that may be brought up concerning the minutes.

It may be better to deal with the car park early on in the meeting but to set a time limit to avoid spending too much time on a minor question.

The results of market research need to be discussed before the other items because this needs to be talked about before a decision can be made to launch the XDLP. If it is launched the budget would probably be discussed before the sales targets. However, you could say that the size of the budget depends on the quantity of sales that is forecast.

The meeting would end with any other business (frequently abbreviated to A.O.B.).

6 Taking part in meetings

A		B
1	Quite honestly	To be frank
2	Actually	In fact
3	Incidentally	By the way
4	If I were you	In your place
5	Broadly speaking	By and large
6	Absolutely	Precisely
7	No way	Out of the question
8	It goes without saying that	Needless to say
9	So	Right

C Suggested answers:

Formal: If I were you/Broadly speaking/
It goes without saying that ...

Neutral: Quite honestly/Actually/Incidentally/
Absolutely/To be frank/By the way/In fact/
Precisely/Needless to say/By and large

Informal: No way/So/Right/Out of the
question/In your place

Tapescript

A: Let's stick to the agenda, shall we? Quite
honestly, I don't really understand why we're
talking about this now.
B: Actually I think it's very important indeed.
I think the Hong Kong market has great
potential. Incidentally, while we're on the
subject, I had a phone call from Mrs Chen the
other day and I took the liberty of telling her that
we were thinking of approaching her on a joint-
venture basis.
A: Now, look John, if I were you, I'd be very
careful what you say. We haven't come to any
kind of decision yet.
C: I tend to agree. I mean broadly speaking,
we try to involve everyone in the decision-
making process and not just act on personal
initiative.
A: Mary thinks we should be looking more
towards Eastern Europe.
D: Absolutely! That's what I've been saying
for years.
C: No way! It just isn't feasible at the moment.
A: Well I think it goes without saying that we're
going to have to get together and talk about this
in more detail, perhaps at the next planning
meeting. (...) So that's settled. Can we now move
on to the next item on the agenda which is ...

7 Reporting what was said

1 raised; **2** accepted; **3** claimed; **4** added;
5 disagreed; **6** argued; **7** replied; **8** advised;
9 admitted; **10** wondered; **11** concluded;
12 recommended

Tapescript

Chairman: I think you had something to say,
Ms Andersson.
Andersson: Yes, thank you. I'd like to bring up
the problem of just-in-time supply procedures.
You've convinced me that they've saved us
a lot of money in warehousing but quite frankly
it seems to me that they actually cause *more*
problems than they solve. Just because Japanese
management procedures are fashionable doesn't
mean to say that we need to follow them blindly.
Deiss: Could I just add a word here, Mr
Chairman?
Chairman: Go ahead, Ms Deiss.
Deiss: I really don't go along with that at all,

Lena. An idea should be judged on its merits,
OK, but I still think that just-in-time procedures
have proved their worth by saving us a great deal
of money.
Andersson: Well, yes, but they've also led to
considerable logistical problems with all the
trucks we have to keep on the road.
Blasetti: I agree with Lena. If it were up to me to
decide I think we should give up on just-in-time.
Chairman: Well, seen from a logistics angle I
have to say that that might be a desirable course
of action but I have my doubts as to the
feasibility, at least in the short term. It'd cost us
a small fortune.
Deiss: I'm not sure the logistics problem
is as bad as you all make out.
Chairman: Right. Thank you, but if I can just
stop you for a moment? It seems to me that,
given the differences in opinion, the best thing
we can do is to adjourn the discussion until we
have figures available. OK? So what I suggest is ...

8 Pronunciation: /e/ /eɪ/ /æ/

B /e/: digression; implement; set; settle; suggest
/eɪ/: arrange; available; circulate; claim; eight;
obtain; participate; raise
/æ/: actually; cancel; fact; frank; matter

9 Learning vocabulary

The ten verbs in the square are: call; cancel;
chair; end; hold; postpone; run; suggest;
suspend; take place

9 Budgets and forecasts

1 Keeping to a budget

A She is basically unhappy and dissatisfied
because she has no control over the budget.

B **1** fixed; **2** targets; **3** meet; **4** allocated;
5 earmarked; **6** revised; **7** exceeded

Tapescript

For us the big problem with budgets is that often
the people who have to work with a budget don't
know how it was fixed or the reasons why,
because they haven't been involved. So when
we have departmental planning meetings with
colleagues, we're not really planning the budget
with them at all. Instead we're sitting down and
informing them about the targets that someone
else has decided and telling them they've got to
meet these targets without spending more than
the sums of money they've been allocated.

All we have to do is keep to the sums that have
been earmarked for expenditure against the
various budget headings – they're not revised if

circumstances change, or anything like that. And if the budget is exceeded we're in a lot of trouble, but it's not really our fault as the figures and the targets have all been set by someone else and in all likelihood not enough money has been earmarked to be able to do the job properly.

All that's left for us to do is to allocate our resources – particularly people in my job, which is sales – but we have no control over goals and very little control over the resources that we actually get. It's very frustrating.

The company's also introduced zero-based budgeting as a means of holding down costs. This means we have to justify spending *any* money at all rather than only having to justify an increase in expenditure as used to be the case. So again we're being kept very much in control and money is tight.

C 1 sums of money; 2 the budget; 3 a target; 4 costs

2 Pronunciation

A Each of them contains the sound /ə/ (known as the schwa) – the most common English vowel sound.

/ˈæləkeɪt/ /ɪnˈtɜːnəl/ /ˈmænɪdʒə/ /ˈmɒnɪtə/ /ˈnʌmbə/ /səˈpəʊz/

B /əˈkaʊntənt/ /əˈnæləsɪs/ /əˈses/ /ˈkæpɪtəl/ /ˈdeɪtə/ /ˈfɪɡə/ /əˈpəʊz/ /ˈpɜːtʃəs/ /kwəʊtə/ /səˈplaɪz/

3 Synonyms: Updating a budget

A A management textbook: it is a technical description of 'budgetary updating' written for someone who is studying the subject.

B 1 variances/differences; 2 requirements/needs
3 checking/monitoring; 4 remedial/corrective
5 review/revise; 6 ensure/guarantee;
7 estimating/guessing; 8 allocating/providing
9 fulfil/achieve; 10 employed/used;
11 expenditure/spending; 12 planned/programmed

4 Easily confused words: check/control

A You **check** something to see if it is correct (or **check on** somebody to see if they are making satisfactory progress). You **control** someone or something if you have power or domination over them.

B 1 checked; 2 beyond our control; 3 check; 4 controlling interest; 5 checked; 6 control

C *Individual answers*

5 Word building

A under-

B overbook; overcharge/undercharge; overdraw; overestimate/underestimate; overpay/underpay; overrate/underrate; overrule; overstock/understock; overvalue/undervalue; overwork

Note that we could also say *underbooked* or *underworked*. But it is not possible to say *underdraw* or *underdrawn*, *underule* or *underuled*.

C *Individual answers*

6 Word puzzle

Horizontal: FIX; MONITOR; REVISE; ESTIMATE; CONTROL; UPDATE; EXPENSE; TARGET; GUESS
Vertical: FORECASTS

7 Synonyms and opposites: Making predictions

A impossible, unlikely, a chance, likely, in all likelihood, a safe bet, bound to, certain

(*Likely* and *in all likelihood* are close in meaning but we feel that the inclusion of the word *all* makes the probability stronger.)

B *Individual answers*

8 Learning vocabulary

Individual answers

10 Describing change

1 Synonyms and opposites: Ups and downs

B risen/climb/reductions

C increased/hike/upward trend

D grew/went up/increases/accelerate/boosted/advance

E plummeted/upturn/strengthen/edging up/weaken/slump

NB: If something 'comes under pressure' it is likely to fall, but these words do not in themselves describe a fall.

2 Synonyms and opposites: Nouns and verbs

A
VERBS

Upward	**Downward**
to pick up	to reduce
to rise	to halve
to climb	to cut
to increase	to slash
to grow	to drop
to go up	to fall
to accelerate	to plummet
to boost	to be down
to strengthen	to weaken
to edge up	

NOUNS

Upward	**Downward**
a hike	a (sharp) fall
an upward trend	a downward trend
an increase	a reduction
an advance	a slump
an upturn	

B Suggested answers:
slump/slash/plummet/hike/accelerate/boost

C
1 a fall; 2 a profit; 3 an advance;
4 an increase; 5 to plummet; 6 to pick up;
7 to halve; 8 to weaken

D Possible answers:
1 is growing; 2 grew/advanced; 3 increased/
grew; 4 went up; 5 increased/grew; 6 dropped;
7 dropped; 8 climbed; 9 was ... down

3 Synonyms and opposites: Verbs and adverbs

A Suggested answer:

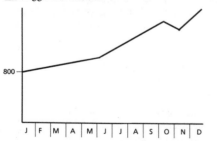

B These sentences do not make sense:
2 (*plummet* is a big change; *marginally* is a very
   small change)
3 (*rocketed* is a big change; *gradually* is a small,
   slow change)
4 (*edged up* is a small, gradual change; *sharply*
   is a big, sudden change)

C Possible combinations:
a sharp fall/drop; a temporary reduction; a slight
upturn/drop/fall; a dramatic rise/fall; a gradual
reduction/rise/fall

4 Prepositions

A 1 ¹ at; ² from; ³ of; ⁴ to; ⁵ over/under; ⁶ to; ⁷ over/under; ⁸ by
2 ¹ by; ² to; ³ of; ⁴ by; ⁵ to

B *Individual answers*

C

🔊 Tapescript
As you can see from the graph, group earnings
rose only slightly from $790m to $810m between
1987 and 1988 owing to the low volume of
consumer spending which, as you will remember,
was caused by continued high interest rates. The
following year they plunged to just under $500m.
I think this particularly dramatic slump in profits
can be put down to some rather badly-planned
diversification moves at that time.

However, earnings fortunately began to grow
again as a result of some necessary restructuring,
at first by a modest $40m in 1990, before soaring
to over $715m the following year. They then
levelled off at around that figure until 1993. This
period of low or zero growth can be accounted
for by the prolonged recession in the UK and
the continued relative weakness of the dollar.
In 1994, however, profits again slumped to
$610m as a consequence of the uncertainty
surrounding our investments in countries with
a high political risk. However, we have survived
and, partly because of the appointment of a new
senior management team, the group began to
perform well again, with profits reaching $812m
in 1995 and $914m in 1997. And next year, with a
bit of luck, we expect to go over the billion mark
for the first time in the company's history.

5 Linking words: Cause and effect

A 2 was caused by; 3 can be put down to;
4 as a result of; 5 can be accounted for by;
6 as a consequence of; 7 (partly) because of
B *Individual answers*

6 Pronunciation: -ough

/əʊ/ although
/ɒf/ trough
/uː/ through
/ʌf/ enough, rough, tough

11 Making presentations

1 Good presentations

Possible answers:
Content/style/voice/manner/the clarity
of the audio-visual aids/lack of hesitation/
confidence/etc.

2 Related words: Visual aids

A 1 screen; 2 whiteboard; 3 monitor;
4 pointer; 5 video recorder; 6 marker pens;
7 transparencies; 8 remote control; 9 OHP;
10 slide projector; 11 slides;
12 flipchart

B *Individual answers*

3 Easily confused words: diagram/graph etc.

A 1 graph; 2 table; 3 bar chart; 4 pie chart;
5 scatter chart; 6 diagram; 7 pictogram

B **a** vertical axis; **b** horizontal axis; **c** curve;
d dotted line; **e** shaded area; **f** segment;
g broken line

4 Pronunciation: Figure work

Check your answers by listening to the cassette.

5 Contrasts and comparisons

1 although; 2 compared with; 3 All the same;
4 Despite; 5 unlike; 6 On the contrary

6 Linking words: Signalling intention

A Rule 1: Assess the risk
Rule 2: Borrow the minimum
Rule 3: Avoid giving credit

Rule 4: Limit your contractual obligations
Rule 5: Don't be over-ambitious
Rule 6: Take out adequate insurance

Sales	£600,000
Gross profit	£540,000
Overheads	£460,000
Profit before interest	£80,000
Interest	£20,000
Net profit	£60,000

Tapescript

A: Look, Michael, time is getting on. Let's get started, shall we?

B: Right, yes. Everyone? Thank you. Well, I'm delighted to welcome Mrs Patel from London Venture Enterprises, who is here to talk to us about how to reduce start-up risks when setting out in one's own business. So, Mrs Patel, over to you.

C: Thank you, Mr Grant. Good afternoon, everyone. Right, my brief this afternoon is to present to you what I see as the six golden rules which you have to remember when setting up in business.

Now, starting a business is inevitably risky – in fact, the average failure rate for new businesses is in the order of 60% within the first three years. So you need to plan to keep the level of risk as low as possible. This means asking yourself 'Has enough research been done for you to know if it can be delivered at a price that will attract enough customers?' After all, a skilled chef may open up a high-class restaurant but only attract customers on a Friday or Saturday night. Or the gross profit may be too little to cover overheads. So, rule one – and here it is on my beautiful OHP transparency – assess the risk.

Um, moving on to the next point, I would like to talk about capitalisation. Let's say a business is capitalised at £200,000 split into £100,000 of the owner's capital and an equal amount in the form of a bank loan. Let's say the bank charges 20% interest, that is to say £20,000 a year. That gives us a forecast something like this – and here I have another wonderful transparency which I hope you can see from the back –

Sales	£600,000
Gross profit	£540,000
Overheads	£460,000
Profit before interest	£80,000
Interest	£20,000
Net profit	£60,000

Of course, you might miss the sales target by, say, 10% or so and if overheads remained unchanged then the situation would be a lot less healthy. So, rule two – plan to borrow the minimum: never more than 50% of the base capital.

A: What about the terms of trade?

C: I'm glad you asked me that, because this brings me to my next point. The main reason for bankruptcy is bad debts. So rule three is – avoid giving credit, and never have a customer who owes you more than 5% of annual turnover.

OK, leaving aside this for the moment because we don't have much time my fourth point is – limit your contractual obligations: for example, avoid taking out a long lease on property before your business has really proved its worth.

Rule five – don't be over-ambitious. Of course, we all start out with great ambitions, but my advice is to avoid incurring overheads at the outset. Rule six – Take out adequate insurance – it's tragic how many small businesses don't cover themselves properly. There's a disaster, a fire or something, and they go to the wall.

So, that's it. Let me recap on what I've said so far. Rule one – assess the risk. Rule two – borrow the minimum. Rule three – avoid giving credit. Rule four – limit your contractual obligations. Rule five – don't be over-ambitious, and rule six – insure your business.

OK. Now, um, if anyone has any questions, I'll be more than happy to try and answer them.

B Opening:
Let's get started, shall we?
I'm delighted to welcome ...
Thank you, x.
Good afternoon, everyone.
Right, so my brief is to ...

Inviting questions:
Now, if anyone has any questions, I'll be more than happy to try and answer them.

Answering questions: I'm glad you asked me that (because) ...

Closing: So that's it.

C *Individual answers*, but other possibilities include:

Opening: I'd like to begin by ...

Inviting questions: Any questions?/Is that clear to everyone?

Answering questions: Yes, that's a (very) good question.

Closing: Well, that's the end of my presentation today. Thank you for listening to me.

D I'm summing up: Let me recap on what I've said so far/In conclusion/So

I'm changing the subject: This brings me to my next point/Moving on to/Leaving this aside for the moment

I'm thinking what to say next: I'm glad you asked me that/Well/Um

7 Making a presentation
Individual answers

8 Learning vocabulary
Possible answer:

12 Personal banking

1 Related words: Banking terms
Across: CREDIT/ACCOUNT/DEPOSIT/ INTEREST/CHEQUE(S)/WITHDRAW
Down: SIGNATURE/PAY/SAFE/ CURRENCIES
Diagonally: SAVINGS/SAVE/DEBIT

2 Related words: Banking services
Individual answers

3 Word associations
branch and *Head Office*: individual branches all report to Head Office
cash dispenser and *withdraw*: you withdraw money from a cash dispenser
credit card and *Visa*: the Visa card is a type of credit card
deposit and *pay in*: these are synonyms
direct debit and *standing order*: these are both ways of making payments automatically
overdrawn and *in the red*: these are synonyms – we use these words to say that an account has a debit balance
payee and *beneficiary*: these are synonyms and refer to the people to whom payment is made
statement and *balance*: when you receive a bank statement you look at the balance to find out your financial position

4 Word partners: Compound nouns
account number; cash flow/point; exchange rate; home banking; income tax; interest rate

5 Pronunciation: Word stress

ac<u>count</u> number; <u>cash flow</u>; <u>cash</u> point; ex<u>change</u>
rate; <u>home banking</u>; <u>income tax</u>; <u>interest rate</u>

6 Colour idioms

1 blue; 2 grey; 3 green; 4 blue ... white; 5 red;
6 blue; 7 black; 8 white

13 Business start-ups

1 Related words: A business plan

A 1 the proposal; 2 the product;
3 the potential market; 4 the financial
projections

B Proposal: blueprint; project; scheme
Territory: area; location; sector
Financial projections: break-even point;
estimate; forecast
Expenses: outgoings; overheads; running costs

2 Word grammar: Multi-word verbs

A back up; bring out; come into; cover up; cut
out; draw up; go about; put by/into; set out/up

formulate – draw up; hide – cover up; highlight –
bring out; inherit – come into; invest – put
(money) into; present – set out; save – put by;
start – set up; suited – cut out; tackle – go about

B 1 run up against; 2 make up for; 3 put up
with; 4 come up to; 5 get down to; 6 do away
with; 7 cut down on

C *Individual answers*

3 Word building: cost

1 cost; 2 costed; 3 costing; 4 costs; 5 at cost
price; 6 to our cost; 7 costly ... cost-effective

4 Franchising

Franchise fee (*training*): £25,000

Fixtures/fittings (*desk, basic office supplies, shelving,
fax, photocopier, answering machine*): £3,000

Computing (*computer, laser printer, software –
database, spreadsheet*): £2,500

Display material (*exhibition stands, leaflets,
brochures, space for advertising in local press*): £1,500

Premises (*rent, legal fees, business rates, local taxes,
insurance, electricity*): £13,500

Working capital: £100,000

Value Added Tax (*at 17.5%*): £17,500

🔊 Tapescript

Rees: OK, I've read your letter and business plan
in which you set out the kind of franchise you're
interested in and it seems a good idea but of
course we've got to get our sums right in advance.
Many people think franchising is going to be a
good idea but in fact underestimate the amount
of capital that really is required.

Franklin: Yes, well, I've brought along some
calculations and I'd like you to give me an idea as
to whether I *have* got my sums right and therefore
whether or not I can afford it.

Rees: Right, well we can perhaps start off by
looking at the outgoings and see how much your
initial working capital should be, and then talk
about how much you have in the way of savings
and then how much the bank could lend you.

Franklin: Right. Well, I've made a kind of
shopping list. Er, the initial franchise fee is
£25,000. That's fixed in advance, and includes
training.

Rees: Yes.

Franklin: Then I thought I would need a sum
of money for fixtures and fittings.

Rees: Yes, you'll probably need a desk, basic
office supplies and shelving.

Franklin: Yes, and I've included provision for
a fax, a photocopier, an answering machine and
that kind of thing. I think something in the
region of £3,000.

Rees: Right, that seems OK.

Franklin: And then I've put down £2,500 under
the heading of computing, so that includes the
purchase of a computer and a printer.

Rees: A laser printer?

Franklin: Yes, I need good quality. And – er –
software – a database and spreadsheet program.

Rees: What about display material?

Franklin: Well, I would need exhibition stands,
and I'd have leaflets and brochures printed for
local distribution and also take out space for
advertising in the local press.

Rees: So that's probably around £1,500 a year.

Franklin: Yes, if not more. And of course I need
premises.

Rees: Have you found anything suitable?

Franklin: Yes, I've got an option on some
premises and I've set aside £12,000 for the first
year's rent plus legal fees of £1,500.

Rees: What about business rates, insurance,
electricity ...?

Franklin: Umm ... yes, I hadn't thought about
that – I'll have to look into that.

Rees: OK, so that leaves us with the working
capital which in this case is something like
£100,000 but on top of that you should make a
provision for VAT. So we'll add that on at 17.5%
which makes ...

5 Pronunciation: /sk/ /ʃ/ /tʃ/

B /sk/: schedule; scheme
/ʃ/: brochure; schedule
/tʃ/: challenge; charge; chart; cheap;
check; franchise

NB: schedule is pronounced /sk/ by American speakers and by many British speakers. It is pronounced /ʃ/ by some British speakers.

6 Learning vocabulary

Suggested links:
highly successful/have made it
company executives/company managers
purchase/buy into
bankroll/finance
funds/venture capital
new/fledgling
borrowing/gearing/loans
equity participation/equity finance
enterprise/venture
danger/risk

14 Investment and finance

1 Related words: Financial terms

A Suggested answers:
A: mergers/acquired/shares
B: (place on the) market/flotation/underwritten
C: profit/losses/dividend (payments)/
turnover/yields

B 1 shares; 2 turnover; 3 dividend/yield;
4 underwritten; 5 acquired; 6 rights
issue/flotation; 7 launched/placed ... on the
market; 8 mergers; 9 losses

2 Word partners: Noun combinations

A 1 market; 2 rate; 3 capital; 4 share

B Suggested answers:

net profit/pre-tax profit/gross profit/operating
profit/healthy profit/make a profit/profit margin

net assets/fixed assets/tangible assets/current
assets/frozen assets/liquid assets/asset stripper

3 Guessing meaning from context

Suggested answers:

A airlines – carriers; plane – aircraft;
drive – campaign; attract – lure;
seats – spaces; on the rise – increasing

B healthy – strong; checks – limiting;
fall – decline

C fall – dropped; giant – huge;
multinational – conglomerate – group;
poor results – disappointing pre-tax profits;
live up to expectations – reach full potential;
sluggish – lethargic

D spurns – flatly rejected – turn down;
offer – takeover bid;
undervalued – does not reflect the true worth;
firm – company

4 Word partners: Compound nouns

A merchant bank; venture capital; credit line;
rights issue; liquid assets; junk bond;
management buyout; insider trading

5 Pronunciation: Letters which are not pronounced

The underlined letters are not pronounced:

clim**b**; de**b**t; forei**g**n; **g**uarantee; hal**f**; mor**t**gage;
recei**p**t; sc**h**eme; **w**holly

6 Raising funds

A 1 debentures (bonds); 2 project financing/
syndicated loan; 3 debentures/factoring

B Suggested answers:

Retained earnings
Advantage: no interest payments
Disadvantage: may not be previous profits to
draw on

Debentures
Advantage: useful for longer-term financing
Disadvantage: must pay interest, whether a profit
is made or not

Factoring
Advantage: guaranteed debt recovery
Disadvantage: have to pay a commission

Project financing
Advantages: large sums can be raised; can finance
individual projects independently; banks share
risk
Disadvantages: none mentioned

Syndicated loans
Advantages: large sums can be raised; banks
share risk; become known in other countries
Disadvantages: none mentioned

🔊 Tapescript
A: So what routes are open to companies that
wish to finance expansion? I suppose one
way would be to generate the funds from past

profits, by retaining earnings instead of distributing them as dividends.

B: Well, yes, and of course that would mean that there would be no interest payments to make, as there are when you borrow money from a bank or issue debentures, but ... er ... self-financing in this way isn't usually possible – for example, a young company simply wouldn't have the previous profits to draw on. No – most companies have to borrow money in some form or other.

A: So what are the options?

B: Well, if we're talking about longer-term financing, that's most frequently obtained through the issue of debentures. These are bonds – that's to say loans made to the company by individual investors – which bear a fixed rate of interest and which mature – that is, are paid back – over a given period of time, say five years. Of course, this means companies always have interest payments
to make, whether they make a profit or not, and this can be a major disadvantage.

A: And are they suitable for all sizes of firm?

B: No, not really, a multinational would probably look to project financing or a syndicated loan.

A: And is there nothing else for a small or medium-sized company?

B: Well, yes. A company can use the services of a factor.

A: Which is?

B: Well, a factor is an intermediary between the company and its customers, where the company invoices its clients in the normal way but gives a copy of all its invoices to the factoring company. The factoring company then recovers all the debts but again the disadvantage is that you have to pay a commission, probably about 10%. What the factor is doing basically is making a loan to the company, which is secured against the value of the invoices.

A: Right. OK, now what about the forms of financing you mentioned for larger-scale operations, project financing and syndicated loans?

B: Yes, well the first one, project financing, is basically self-explanatory. What it does is allow a particular project – especially large-scale construction schemes, such as the Channel Tunnel, for instance – to be financed independently of other commitments and so for the company concerned there are two big advantages: the financing of the project is independent from other projects the company is involved in, and the banks lending the money share some of the risk. The lender looks at the project and assesses the return on the investment and if it seems like a good risk, then the bank participates.

A: And a syndicated loan, what's that?

B: Well, if the sum is more than any one bank

is willing to lend, then several banks – a syndicate – will contribute.

A: So you can in fact raise large sums in this way because the risk is shared?

B: That's right, and another advantage for the borrower is that your name becomes known, and quite often with overseas banks this can lead to useful banking contacts in countries where you may have plans to expand.

C *Individual answers*

7 Related words: Financial ratios

1 return on investment; **2** earnings per share;
3 working capital ratio; **4** debt-equity ratio
5 price-earnings ratio

8 Learning vocabulary

A The following compound nouns can be generated, among others:

equity capital; gross profit; net capital; net loss; net profit; share capital; takeover bid; working capital

The following verb and noun combinations are possible:
launch a bid; launch a flotation; raise capital; raise funds; yield a profit

Gross and net, profit and loss are opposites.

B Sample sentences:
You need to raise funds to launch a takeover bid.
If you want to make a profit from your investment you must look carefully at the earnings per share.

15   Export payments

1 Related words: Documentation

B **1** air waybill; **2** import licence;
3 consular invoice; **4** pro-forma invoice;
5 irrevocable letter of credit; **6** sight draft;
7 insurance certificate

2 Abbreviations

A B/L = bill of lading; AWB = air waybill;
L/C = letter of credit

B @ = at (when stating a unit price)
a/c = account
ASAP = as soon as possible
B/E = bill of exchange
COD = cash on delivery
IOU = I owe you
NB = *nota bene* (= 'note carefully' in Latin)

RSVP = *répondez s'il vous plaît* (= 'please reply' in French)
SWIFT = Society for Worldwide Inter-Bank Financial Telecommunications
VAT = value added tax

C 1 SWIFT; 2 ASAP; 3 RSVP; 4 VAT; 5 a/c; 6 @; 7 NB; 8 COD; 9 IOU; 10 B/E

3 Linking words: Sequencing (1)

1 H; 2 J; 3 A; 4 F; 5 C; 6 D; 7 I; 8 L; 9 K; 10 E; 11 B; 12 G

Tapescript

How does a documentary credit work? Well, first of all, there has to be a sales contract between a producer and an exporter, and this sales contract must contain an arrangement for payment through a documentary credit.

Secondly, the importing company instructs its bank to provide a credit line – in other words to prepare this documentary credit in the producer's – that is, the exporter's – favour. Because this is the bank that issues the documentary credit, it is known as the *issuing* bank. At this point the issuing bank asks a bank – usually the producer's own bank – in the producer's country to confirm the credit line by telling – the technical word is to advise – the producer that the credit has been drawn up. For this reason, this bank – the producer's – is known as the *advising* bank. This advising bank then sends the producer – who is also the exporter – the credit, and when this has been done the exporter sends the goods to the importer.

After this, the exporter presents the documents to a bank – normally the advising bank, which checks them to see they are in order, and then pays the exporter. Next, the documents are forwarded or sent to the issuing bank in the importer's own country. The issuing bank checks them again before reimbursing the advising bank. It is at this stage that the importing company pays the issuing bank the amount due, usually by simple debit. Finally, the issuing bank releases the documents to the importer, who uses them to obtain delivery of the goods.

4 Word partners: Verbs and nouns

1 release/present/check/forward the documents
2 despatch/take delivery of the goods
3 conclude a contract
4 arrange a payment
5 advise /confirm/provide a credit line

5 Linking words: Sequencing (2)

Possible answer:
First of all, a British exporter and an overseas buyer conclude a sales contract with payment to be arranged by documentary credit. **Secondly** the overseas buyer tells the issuing bank to provide a credit line in favour of the exporter. **At this stage** the issuing bank asks the UK bank to advise and/or confirm the credit line. **Next** the UK advising/confirming bank sends the letter of credit to the exporter. **After this** the exporter despatches the goods to the overseas buyer. **When this has been done** the exporter presents the shipping documents to the bank holding the credit, i.e. the UK advising/confirming bank **and** the UK bank checks the documents, pays and/or accepts under the terms of the credit. **At this point** the UK advising/confirming bank forwards the documents to the issuing bank. The issuing bank **then** checks the documents and reimburses the UK bank. **Next** the overseas buyer is debited by the issuing bank in a previously agreed manner. The issuing bank **then** releases the documents to the foreign buyer. **Finally**, with the documents in his possession, the overseas buyer takes delivery of the goods.

6 Pronunciation: Letters and numbers

1 Flight Number SR843 to Zürich ETA 11.05
2 GA/54493 YP
3 Account number 200 222 53
  Branch number 03051
4 File number 0093–237–7955: 13 March
5 C/N O1 Pan American Container care of A-Z. G & W International Forwarders Inc. FH 888

Tapescript

1 OK so that's flight number SR843 to Zürich with an ETA of 11.05.
2 And our reference number is GA/54493 YP.
3 That's account number 200 222 53 and the branch number is 03051.
4 The file number is 0093–237–7955 and it's dated the 13th of March.
5 There are some marks and numbers on the Bill of Lading; it says C/N O1 and then Pan American Container care of A-Z. and the forwarding agent is G & W International Forwarders Inc. and their reference is FH triple eight.

7 Prepositions of time: in/on/by/at/within

A *in* a week: after a specific period of time
at six o'clock: a particular moment
by the end of the month: before the end of
a stated period of time
on Friday 21 May: a specific day or date
within two weeks: before or on a specific day,
date or time

in due course; *by* this time next …;
at the latest; *at* short notice; *at* the earliest;
on request; *on* arrival; *by* return of mail;
in advance; *on* schedule; *on* delivery

C 1 by … at; 2 in; 3 on; 4 within; 5 at;
6 by; 7 in … on

8 Easily confused words: in time/on time

A *in time* = before it is too late
on time = at the exact time that was expected

B 1 in time; 2 on time; 3 on time; 4 in time

16 Complaining and apologising

1 Related words: Consumer preferences

Individual answers

2 Word building: Prefixes

A They all mean 'not'.

B faulty = imperfect
insufficient = inadequate
rude = impolite
unbearable = intolerable
unhappy = dissatisfied
unjust = unfair
unpleasant = disagreeable
unsympathetic = unhelpful

C Possible answers:
faulty/imperfect – to describe a product
insufficient/inadequate – to describe the
compensation that you were offered
rude/impolite/unsympathetic/unhelpful – to
describe people, especially sales staff
unhappy/dissatisfied – to describe your own
feelings about the quality of a product, or how
you were treated
unjust/unfair/unbearable/intolerable – to
describe the reactions of the sales staff
unpleasant/disagreeable – to describe an
experience; something that has happened to you

3 Spelling: Suffixes -ence/-ance

acceptance; assistance; assurance; conference;
insistence; maintenance; occurrence; performance;
persistence; preference; reference; remittance

4 Pronunciation: Word stress

A The second syllable

B The syllable before the *-ance/-ence*

The words often pronounced with only
two syllables are:

conference /ˈkɒnfrəns/
preference /ˈprefrəns/
reference /ˈrefrəns/

The stress is on the first syllable.

5 Related words: Making complaints

A *Individual answers*

B A: polite, firm; B: polite, furious; C: polite,
firm; D: polite, furious.

C fax A: conversation 3; fax B: conversation 1;
fax C: conversation 4; fax D: conversation 2.

D Suggested answers:
Contracts: renewal; penalty clause

Payment: indemnity; remittance; settle;
statement; cheque; (issue) credit; balance;
invoice

Delivery: late; ship; mishandling; dispatch
(goods)

Maintenance: after-sales service; break down;
(routine) service; service engineer

🔊 Tapescript
Conversation 1
A: Good morning, can I speak with Kenneth T
Zick, please?
B: I'm very sorry, Mr Zick is in conference right
now. Would you like to leave a message?
A: Yes, could you tell him that Mr Caudillo
phoned from Southern Cigars and wanted to
speak with him about the 74 adhesive rolls he
bought from us in April of this year and has just
returned. Almost half had already been used and
three weren't even ours. Under the circumstances
he really can't expect us to issue a credit note for
futher purchases.
B: OK, I've got that, Mr Caudillo. I'll give him
the message as soon as I can.
A: Thank you.

Conversation 2
A: Brookes.
B: Hello, Mr Brookes, this is Monica Armstrong

of Northern Engineering.

A: Ah yes, Mrs Armstrong ...

B: As you've probably guessed, I'm calling about the order which should have arrived a couple of weeks ago and that we're still waiting for. It's not the first time I've had to complain about your late deliveries, but this really is the last straw; we've even had to cut production. Now either you do something to improve your performance or we find a new supplier!

Conversation 3

A: Eznack speaking.

B: Good morning, Mr Eznack, this is Malcolm McDonald in Glasgow.

A: Ah yes, Mr McDonald, what can I do for you?

B: I'm calling about the machine parts which should have arrived today.

A: You mean they haven't arrived yet?

B: No, they haven't, and I'd just like to say this. If it was the first time this kind of thing had happened, it would be bad enough, but it's far from the case ...

A: Mr McDonald, I assure you ...

B: I'm sorry, I don't want your assurances, I want my parts. In the meantime, I expect to receive both them and the penalty clause payment within the next few days ...

A: Of course, Mr McDonald, but ...

B: But nothing! And if I don't see marked improvement very soon, I'll be looking at new suppliers. Goodbye, Mr Eznack.

Conversation 4

A: After-sales. Can I help you?

B: Yes, this is Ulla Schultz from APAG in Hamburg. I'm calling because we are concerned about the standard of after-sales service your German office is offering. I believe we're one of your biggest customers in Germany, and I'm afraid we cannot afford and do not intend to afford the service delays you're imposing.

A: Well Ms Schultz, I'm extremely concerned to hear about ...

6 Easily confused words: remind/remember

A You remind *someone* (about something) You remember *something*.

B *Individual answers*

C *Individual answers*

7 Apologies

A *Individual answers*

B Fax C

C (extremely) sorry ... (sincerely) apologise

D Fax A

1 sorry; **2** resolved; **3** apologise; **4** inconvenience; **5** assure; **6** prompt; **7** returned to normal

17 Information systems

1 A communications crossword

Horizontal: E-MAIL; SCREEN; FAX; FREEFONE; RECORD; MODEM; MESSAGE; SPREADSHEET; FILE; SOFTWARE; NETWORK
Vertical: INFORMATION

2 Pronunciation: Stress in compound nouns

answerphone   phone call

display screen   photocopier

feedback   photocopy

laser printer   spreadsheet

message pad   training course

3 Word grammar: Noun combinations

A 1 ✓; 2 ✓; 3 ✗; 4 ✗; 5 ✓; 6 ✓; 7 ✗; 8 ✗; 9 ✗; 10 ✗

B the function of the mailroom; voice mail; (every) manager's desktop computer; security clearance; password; paper filing systems; Murphy's law

4 Related words: Equipment

1 a mobile phone; **2** a car phone; **3** a radiopager; **4** an OCR scanner; **5** an electronic notepad; **6** a multimedia videophone

🖙 Tapescript

1 It's quite good, except that there are only 30 characters on the screen so it's a bit difficult to read. But I can store 99 numbers in the memory and I can intercept a call by pressing any key. There are a couple of batteries and they give me about 80 minutes' talking time.

2   I find it very useful because I travel a lot. It's voice-activated so I don't have to take my hands off the wheel. I just speak the name of the person I want to call and it dials the number for me.

3   It's called a Message Master. If I'm somewhere off-site then it bleeps and I know I have to make a call back to the office. I can actually turn the sound off if, for example, I'm in a meeting and then read up to 40 messages which are stored in the memory. I wouldn't be without it.

4   I used to have to key in a lot of documents but now the computer does it for me. It makes a kind of photocopy of the page and then with optical character software it's converted from a picture into text, which I can then change if I like on my word processor.

5   It's flat, it fits into the palm of your hand, it doesn't have a keyboard or a handset, just a kind of electronic pen. You write on the screen and it recognises your handwriting and then automatically organises what you've written – let's say 'lunch with Mr Tanaka on March 25' – into your schedule and checks that you haven't made any other appointments at the same time. You can hook it up to a phone line or a computer and use it as a fax or as a pager.

6   I can call up my correspondent without leaving the computer and see him or her on part of the screen at the same time as we talk. It makes a telephone call much less impersonal. And when we've finished talking I can send that person a fax or e-mail or transfer electronic data to a workstation on the other side of the world, again without leaving my terminal.

5 Related words: Processing data

A **1** storage media; **2** the input phase; **3** information processing; **4** the output phase; **5** feedback

B Possible extra words and expressions:

Storage media: microfiche; OHP transparencies; slides; film; cassette tape

The input phase: receiving a phone call

Information processing: creating a database and keying in data

The output phase: mailing a letter; sending a telex

Feedback: returned questionnaires

C *Individual answers*

End of Key

Index

Introduction

Each word in the index has its pronunciation indicated in phonetic script. Not everybody is familiar with phonetic script so you may find the guide below helpful.

Pronunciation

As you know, there are many different varieties of English and we cannot say there is one absolute standard of pronunciation. However, the phonetic transcriptions we have made will enable you to be understood by the vast majority of speakers of English around the world.

In order to pronounce a word acceptably you need to know that words are divided into syllables. For example: help (1 syllable) help•ful (2 syllables) un•help•ful (3 syllables)

Stress

Placed before a syllable, the symbol ' indicates the main stress in a word. In words of more than one syllable it is important to know where to put the stress (i.e. which syllable is given extra force). For example: stra'tegic e'conomy Ja'pan

Long vowel sounds

A colon (:) means that the vowel sound is relatively long. For example: /iː/ sleep me /ɜː/ turn bird work

Vowels		Consonants	
Symbol	Example	Symbol	Example
/iː/	eat	/p/	pull
/i/	happy (found at the end of words)	/b/	bag
/ɪ/	bill	/t/	two
/ʊ/	pull	/d/	drop
/uː/	two	/f/	fall
/e/	met	/v/	visa
/ə/	arrive	/θ/	thick
/ɜː/	her	/ð/	breathe
/ɔː/	four	/m/	man
/æ/	black	/n/	no
/ʌ/	cut	/ŋ/	sing
/ɑː/	far	/h/	hot
/ɒ/	hot	/tʃ/	chip
/ɪə/	here	/dʒ/	judge
/eɪ/	pay	/k/	cut
/ʊə/	poor	/s/	sell
/ɔɪ/	boy	/z/	zero
/eə/	air	/ʃ/	share
/aɪ/	eye	/l/	last
/əʊ/	no	/r/	run
/aʊ/	now	/w/	wait
		/j/	you
		/g/	go
		/ʒ/	usual